Columbia University

Contributions to Education

Teachers College Series

No. 270

AMS PRESS
NEW YORK

THE LEGAL STATUS OF CITY SCHOOL BOARDS

BY

GROVER CLEVELAND MOREHART

SUBMITTED IN PARTIAL FULFILLMENT OF THE REQUIREMENTS FOR THE DEGREE OF DOCTOR OF PHILOSOPHY IN THE FACULTY OF PHILOSOPHY, COLUMBIA UNIVERSITY

BUREAU OF PUBLICATIONS
Teachers College, Columbia University
NEW YORK CITY
1927

Library of Congress Cataloging in Publication Data

Morehart, Grover Cleveland, 1885-
The legal status of city school boards.

Reprint of the 1927 ed., issued in series: Teachers College, Columbia University. Contributions to education, no. 270.
Originally presented as the author's thesis, Columbia.
Bibliography: p.
1. School boards--United States. 2. School management and organization--Law and legislation--United States. I. Title. II. Series: Columbia University. Teachers College. Contributions to education, no. 270.
KF4131.Z9M67 1972 344'.73'073 78-177082
ISBN 0-404-55270-6

Reprinted by Special Arrangement with Teachers College Press, New York, New York

From the edition of 1927, New York
First AMS edition published in 1972
Manufactured in the United States

AMS PRESS, INC.
NEW YORK, N. Y. 10003

ACKNOWLEDGMENTS

The writer very gratefully acknowledges his indebtedness to Professor N. L. Engelhardt for proposing the subject of this investigation and for giving numerous helpful suggestions during its prosecution. He wishes, also, to acknowledge his indebtedness to Professors E. H. Reisner, J. R. McGaughy and Paul Mort for assistance given.

G. C. M.

CONTENTS

TABLES AND DIAGRAMS

THE LEGAL STATUS OF CITY SCHOOL BOARDS

CHAPTER I

INTRODUCTION

THE PROBLEM

Throughout the nation many city school boards are in difficulties because they do not know what they legally can do or cannot do. There is, consequently, a need for determining the legal status of the city school board. But this problem is only an integral part of a more general problem. This general problem is to ascertain those conditions of state and local organization which are absolutely necessary to encourage educational progress in the greatest degree possible. One of the several aspects of this broad, general problem is to determine those strictly legal conditions which are most likely to accelerate such educational progress in city school systems.

The importance of the legal aspects of the larger educational problem has been apparent for some time to the educational profession. The following statements are evidence thereof.

"It is often said that there are after all only about three major problems in state school administration. The first is that of securing a proper form of educational organization—one under which real and substantial progress can be made.[1] *

"The growth of school education in entire sections of the country has been retarded because of bad school organization; while other sections, less fortunately situated in other ways, have been able to make exceptional progress in school reorganization because favored by modern laws on this subject."[2]

THE ATTACK AND TREATMENT OF THE PROBLEM

The most promising set-up of the specific problem of determining the legal status of city school boards has been found to

* Numbers refer to references in Appendix III.

be: first, to discover the present status; and, second, to use the most promising available criteria to evaluate the existing legal provisions. This done, it is permissible to offer those legal principles and provisions indicated as of most intrinsic worth as good potential practice in school code drafting.

The natural order for the treatment of the first phase of this task is to analyze the legal sources having to do with the creation and present status of the school district and of school district action. Such analyses disclose the origin, present varieties of organization, the legal nature of the district, and the principles which support its acts. It classes the district as a creation and an agent of the state legislature and thereby indicates the source, extent, and nature of the district's power.

A like analysis of the city school board discloses its source, legal nature, limitations, and present status.

Since both districts and boards of education are created by the state codes or statutes, and will be affected as to efficiency by the nature of such legislation, it becomes a proper phase of this study to compile the principles of code development, and to discuss the factors underlying the making and growth of school codes. This naturally leads to the sources, the criteria of worth, the factors that operate to stratify or set them in varying degrees of inelasticity, administerial problems, final objectives, and so forth.

With this basic information as to the sources, nature and purposes of law, the next phase of this study is to select from available sources those legal principles and provisions which would foster the greatest educational growth. To make this selection, certain criteria are necessary, by the application of which the value of any present or proposed legal principle or provision can be judged.

CRITERIA OF VALUES

After considering the frequency of occurrence of a principle in the several state codes, present tendencies of legislation, specific legislation of states generally believed to be most progressive, it seemed best to use the results of research and expert opinion as set forth in the many city school surveys as the most scientific criteria of worth for judging principles and proposals for educational legal practice. This research and expert opinion is found to cover the field of legal practice in regard to schools in a surprisingly exhaustive manner. Furthermore, the almost universal agreement among the many surveyors, on practically every phase of the legal requirements of a dynamic school program, is an impressive index of the intrinsic worth of the principles advocated.

From these principles, chosen because indicated by research and expert opinion, and by the analyses of the school codes of the several states, a checking list has been drafted. Against this checking list the laws of any state may be checked. This would determine, by comparison at least, whether or not the laws of the state so checked conform to those legal conditions which this study has indicated as the best practice.

SUGGESTED ACT IN APPENDIX I

Appended to the study is a suggested act. It is hoped that this suggested act may be valuable as a guide to legislators and to legal counsel in educational affairs. The writer is not unmindful of the possible objection that he has projected his own judgment too far in proposing this codification. But it must be remembered that the legislator attempts to do the same thing without access to anything like the rich material that has constantly been before the writer. Furthermore, the legislator's efforts, if enacted, go into practice, even though they are but the product of empirical knowledge, lacking, of necessity, scientific evaluation. Time and failure are the checks against the legislator's mistakes. To help eliminate just such sources of danger, this act is suggested.

CHAPTER II

DISTRICTS AND PRINCIPLES OF DISTRICT ACTION

THE DISTRICT: GENERAL CLASSIFICATION OF ITS FUNCTIONS

School districts are agencies of the state legislatures,[1] * created for the express purpose of managing the local schools.[2] As such agencies they are endowed by their respective creators with certain definitely specified, and some more or less implied powers.[3] Some of these powers are to be delegated by the district to their respective boards and other officers. Other powers and duties are inherent in the district and cannot be delegated; but they must be exercised only by ascertaining, in some way, the will of the majority of the legally enfranchised electors of the district. Of these functions, which, with very rare exceptions, must be performed as a direct act of the district, the chief ones are:

1. Meeting, organizing, and transacting business.
2. The election of a board of education.
3. The determination of general policies.

Whenever (1) and (2) are given by the legislature to the district they can seldom, if ever, be delegated; but, the prevailing practice in regard to (3) shows a very great variation in the several states, both in the degree of the power enjoyed and in the number of functions exercised directly by the district.

DETERMINATION OF POLICY

The following outline will show at a glance the scope of the powers which are more or less frequently prescribed in the law as of (3)—the determination of general policies,—to be the direct action of the district in regular or special meetings. Of course, it must be remembered that no one state necessarily

* Numbers refer to references in Appendix III.

directs that each and every one of these functions is to be performed directly by the district; nor is it likely that any two states have identical practice in these matters. But the authority to determine the policies enumerated in the outline is often enough conferred upon the district to justify placing them in the given form as indicative of the scope of the district's possible activities.

The district's possible powers in the determination of general policies concerning:

A. Acquisition and disposal of property:
   1. To purchase sites.
   2. To lease sites.
   3. To purchase buildings.
   4. To lease buildings.
   5. To erect buildings.
   6. To sell or otherwise dispose of real property.

B. Control or management of property:
   1. To authorize the repair of buildings or other property.
   2. To improve sites, pave, beautify, fence, wall, etc.
   3. To procure, direct the use of, or dispose of personal property.

C. Control of the size of the school system by vote to:
   1. Add one or more high schools.
   2. Add one or more junior high schools.
   3. Establish and maintain a municipal college or university.
   4. Add one or more kindergartens.
   5. Set aside playgrounds and other recreational features.
   6. Establish and maintain district libraries.
   7. Hire teachers, conductors and other employees.
   8. Discontinue any or all of the above.

D. Control over the size of the district:
   1. By adding territory.
   2. By dropping territory.
   3. By union of districts or parts thereof.

E. Control by vote over change in the organization of the board of education, or that of other offices:
   1. As to numbers.
   2. As to function.
   3. As to title.

F. Control of a fiscal nature by vote to:
   1. Increase taxes or tax rates.
   2. Decrease taxes or tax rates; or, to adjust them between the low and high levels set by legislation.
   3. Bond the district. This can seldom be done except by popular vote of the district, and more especially if the bonds are for an extension of school indebtedness. As a rule the state laws specify the maximum per cent of the total assessed valuation for which the district may vote to issue bonds, and the method to be provided for payment of principal and interest.

G. Vote to delegate any or all of the above named powers to their lawfully constituted boards.

THE FUNCTIONS OF THE DISTRICT CONSIDERED CHRONOLOGICALLY

This study now considers the activities of the district separately and somewhat in detail. Chronologically, the first step is to meet and perfect an organization for the purpose of transacting the necessary business in the proper form as prescribed in the law, or, in case this form is not so prescribed, to abide by the precedents of the district, or those of similar districts, or to follow some standard set of rules of order.

The second step is the selection of a board or other agency to act for the district between the regular or special meetings of the district.

The third and most important function is to determine the general policies which the law directs the district to determine, or, in case it does not so direct, to perform as the district's business those tasks which the traditions and records of former meetings, both of the district in question and of similar districts of the state, indicate as the practice and the official business of such meetings.

The matter of organization is uniformly quite a formal proceeding and has no particular interest for this study. The same is true to a somewhat less degree in the matter of determination of general policies. So far as it needs to be understood at this point, the preceding outline will afford the required information. The matter of selection of a board by the district is the more immediate concern of this study.

THE LEGISLATURE'S CONTROL OF DISTRICTS

All school districts and all school boards are creatures of the state legislatures. That is, neither the district nor the board exists by virtue of the federal or the state constitutions. The state legislatures have created both of them to facilitate such legislatures in fulfilling their constitutional obligations to provide a system of free schools for the public. Such an obligation, or mandatory clause, is to be found in all of the state constitutions. And since the schools must obviously exist in all parts of the state, thereby making personal control by the legislature practically impossible, it is evident that there must likewise exist some sort of agency to take over the actual, local management of them.

To meet this effectively the legislatures have created agencies in the nature of districts with *quasi* corporate powers, and have given them control of the schools.[3] To direct these agencies, the legislatures almost universally have specified that the official, continuous business of the district shall be conducted by boards, variously designated in the several states. Thus, a sort of agency within an agency, or a "subagency", is the result, both coming into being and continuing to exist by legal enactment of the state legislature.

But since a legislative branch of government can repeal its own acts it follows, of course, that the legislature may discontinue, diminish, or enlarge the size of a district, curtail or increase its powers, change slightly or radically the form and rules for its government, or, in a word, mold the destiny of a district as it wills.

It is evident, then, that should the legislature choose to do so it might name, directly, the members of the local school boards and fix their legal status. In fact the courts of last resort have upheld this very action of a state as constitutional.[4] The legislature of Maryland vests the power in the governor to appoint a county school commissioner, and this commissioner appoints a board of local trustees. The duties of these trustees are nominal or very petty. This is, perhaps, a case of as nearly direct control by the legislature as we have. Quite generally, however, local boards which exercise large powers over the schools have been created by the legislatures.

METHODS OF SELECTION OF BOARDS BY DISTRICTS

The city boards of education are selected by a variety of methods among which are:

1. Election by popular vote.[5]
2. Election by city council, board of commissioners, or other city government officials.[6]
3. Appointment by the mayor or city manager.[7]
4. Appointment by the court of common pleas.[8]
5. And by a self-perpetuating system whereby the remaining members of the board elect successors to those whose terms have expired or terminated in any other manner.[9]

RANGE IN THE NUMBER AND RESPONSIBILITIES OF MEMBERS OF BOARDS OF EDUCATION

The number of members ranges from none or no board at all in St. Paul, Minnesota, to 33 (1921) in Providence, Rhode Island. The median number was five in 1923. There has long been a prevalent tendency to have one or more special members occupy clerical positions of some sort, most often being designated as "clerk," "secretary," and "treasurer." In most states they have no vote or voice in the official business of the board. But in a few states their responsibilities are greater, so that the total range is from that of a stenographic clerk to full rights and duties of regular members, including the right to vote on all questions.

THE RECENT TREND TOWARD A SMALLER BOARD OF EDUCATION

During the last two decades there has been a tendency to cut down the number of memberships on the larger boards and a lesser tendency to raise or increase the number on boards that have had less than five members.[10] These movements, however, have not changed the median number of regular members. It is, perhaps, fortunate that these are the tendencies, for the evidence is rapidly becoming more convincing that a board of five members, all things considered, is better than one of any other size. It is thought by some authorities that a small board of five members will attract the best personnel; [11] the small board will confine its activities to legislation and leave the administration of the schools in the hands of experts,[12] while the larger board will be compelled by its own unwieldiness to create many standing committees;[13] the small board can be seated about a small table and discuss the business informally, thus avoiding the dangers of oratorical discussion and of mob psychology.[14] Doubtless these considerations have been the causes of the tendency toward a small board rather than the recognized benefits from the movement. In fact the leading authorities on educational administration have long since foreseen the advantages of a small board and have vigorously championed the idea.[15] Their advice has evidently been taken seriously wherever it has been heard and fully appreciated, with the consequent result that we have been experiencing for some years a decided trend toward the smaller board of education in cities throughout the several states.

The following table shows the number of members, the length of the term of office, and the manner of their selection, in the most important groups of cities governed by the general laws of the several states.

TABLE I

SHOWING NUMBER OF MEMBERS, LENGTH OF TERM, AND MANNER OF SELECTION OF CITY BOARDS AS PROVIDED FOR IN THE STATUTES OF THE RESPECTIVE STATES, 1923

Index Number of the States	States	Number of Members	Length of Term	How Selected
1	Alabama	5	5	City council
2	Arizona	3	3	Elected at large
3	Arkansas	6	3	Elected at large
4	California	3	3	Elected at large
5	Colorado	5	6	Elected at large
6	Connecticut	3, 6, 9, 12	3	Elected at large
7	Delaware	3	3	Elected at large
8	Florida *			
9	Georgia *			
10	Idaho	3	3	Elected at large
11	Illinois	15	3	Elected at large
12	Indiana	3, 5, 7	3	City council; mayor
13	Iowa	7	3	Elected at large
14	Kansas	6	3	Elected at large
15	Kentucky	5, 9	4	Elected at large
16	Louisiana	5, 9	6	Elected by parish
17	Maine	3	3	Elected at large
18	Maryland *			

* County organization.

TABLE I (*Continued*)

Index Number of the States	States	Number of Members	Length of Term	How Selected
19	Massachusetts	Any multiple of 3	3	Elected at large
20	Michigan	6	3	Elected at large
21	Minnesota	6	3	Elected at large
22	Mississippi	5	3	Mayor and council
23	Missouri	6	3	Elected at large
24	Montana	7	3	Elected at large
25	Nebraska	6	3	Elected at large
26	Nevada	5	3	Elected at large
27	New Hampshire	3, 6, 8	3	Elected at large
28	New Jersey	5, 9	3	Mayor
29	New Mexico	5	4	Elected at large
30	New York	3, 6–9	3, 5	Elected; mayor
31	North Carolina †			
32	North Dakota	7	3	Elected at large
33	Ohio	5, 7, 9	4	Elected at large
34	Oklahoma	2–10	4	Elected by wards
35	Oregon	5	3	Elected at large
36	Pennsylvania	5–15	6	Common pleas court; elected
37	Rhode Island	3	3	Elected at large
38	South Carolina	9	6	Elected at large
39	South Dakota	5	3	Elected at large
40	Tennessee	6	3	Mayor and council
41	Texas	7	2	Elected at large
42	Utah	10	4	Elected by wards
43	Vermont	(each ward) 3	3	Elected at large
44	Virginia	(each ward) 3	3	City council
45	Washington	5	3	Elected at large
46	West Virginia ††			
47	Wisconsin	7–15	3	Elected; appointed
48	Wyoming	6	3	Elected at large

† No general law; 149 charter districts.
†† Charter districts only.

Table II gives further evidence of the trend toward the smaller board of education. Data are presented on the 28 cities of the United States which had a population of 100,000 people, or more, in 1890. The table indicates clearly that in the two decades, 1893-1913, there was a very decided tendency from the large to the small board of education in our largest cities. Also, it is evident that, while greatly slowed up, the movement is still noticeable in the decade 1913-1923. The greatest reductions in the last of these three decades are seen to be those of New York City and Detroit. This would indicate that the "after-growth" was not caused by backward communities adopting a policy long after larger and more progressive cities had abandoned as obsolete the older practice.

ELIGIBILITY FOR MEMBERSHIP ON BOARDS OF EDUCATION

Men have always been eligible as board members. Women were eligible in many states prior to the Nineteenth Amendment and in all states since its adoption. The legal fiction underlying the granting of the suffrage and eligibility to office in school affairs to women while they were denied the ballot in other matters is that school boards are creatures of the legislatures while all political officials are creatures of the state constitutions. This gives the legislature the sole right to say who may vote for school members, while to have given equal rights of suffrage in all

TABLE II

SHOWING CHANGES—DURING PERIOD OF THIRTY YEARS, 1893-1923—IN THE NUMBER OF BOARD MEMBERS IN THE 28 CITIES OF THE UNITED STATES HAVING 100,000 POPULATION IN 1890

CITIES	1893	1913	1923
New York City	21	46	7
Brooklyn *	45	..	..
Chicago	21	21	11
Philadelphia	37	15	15
St. Louis	21	12	12
Boston	24	5	5
Baltimore	23	9	7
San Francisco	12	4	7
Cincinnati	30	7	7
Cleveland	7	7	7
Buffalo	..	..	5
New Orleans	20	5	5
Pittsburgh	37	15	15
Allegheny †	78	..	..
Washington	9	9	9
Detroit	16	21	7
Milwaukee	36	15	15
Newark	30	9	9
Minneapolis	7	7	7
Jersey City	7	9	9
Louisville	24	5	5
Omaha	15	12	12
Rochester, New York	20	5	5
St. Paul ††	7	7	..
Kansas City	6	6	6
Providence	33	3	33
Denver	6	5	7
Indianapolis	11	5	5
Totals	603	264	232

* Incorporated with New York City before 1913.
† Incorporated with Pittsburgh before 1913.
†† One commissioner in 1923.

matters would have required an amendment to the constitution.[16] In a few states equal suffrage was written into the constitution,[17] in others it was embodied in an amendment to the constitution,[18] but in most states there was too much opposition to it for its passage, based on the fear that women voters would outlaw the liquor business.

In addition to sex, there are other more or less frequently mentioned qualifications for membership on city boards. Among them are: age, ranging from 21 in most states to 30 years in Kentucky; residence in the state, the city and the district; citizenship in the United States and thereby in the local state; ownership of property; paying taxes; parentage; guardianship; being head of the family; being the wife of a citizen, property owner, taxpayer, or parent; greater age than 21 years; the ability to read and write; being a regularly qualified elector of the district; being of good moral character; being a discreet and judicious person. Thus the legislatures by statutes have prescribed the qualifications for membership on boards of education, so that it is merely a matter of time, tenor, and temper of the legislatures which have determined the number and the nature of the qualification.

SPECIFIC POLICIES DETERMINED BY SCHOOL DISTRICTS

The third of the major functions frequently exercised by the district is the determination of certain fundamental policies. Among these are:

1. The exercise of certain property rights.
2. The determination of the scope of the schools.[19]
3. Control over the size of the district.[20]
4. Mandates on tax levies.[21]
5. Financial direction.
6. Control over school activities.[22]
7. Delegation of any one or all of the above named functions to the district board or to a special committee.[23]

The degree to which these functions are exercised by the district seems to depend in large measure upon two conditions:

1. The age of the laws in operation.
2. Whether or not the district is operating under the so-called "town" system, or some system closely resembling it.

In New England the district meeting is empowered, and it is its duty to exercise these powers of determination of policy to a very large extent. This is likewise true in some parts of the South and in parts of the old Northwest Territory.

THE DELEGATION OF POWERS TO BOARDS OF EDUCATION

But in the newer states and in those states where the whole school code has recently been revamped, the tendency is to confer or delegate, in very large degree, powers exercised by the district under the "town" system, to the legally constituted board of education. Outside of New England, the actual execution of these functions is, with so few exceptions as to be predominantly the practice, designated as powers and duties of the board of education. And they are left in large measure to the board's discretion, so far as the method of execution is concerned.

But even beyond the confines of New England the law quite generally provides, where otherwise not obligatory, that the board may at its option submit many of these questions to a direct vote of the people. On the other hand, the board may quite generally be compelled to submit certain issues to a vote of the electorate when petitioned to do so by the voters or the freeholders of the district.

THE OBJECTIVE OF THE LEGAL OBLIGATIONS IMPOSED UPON SCHOOL DISTRICTS

In concluding this chapter on district action it will be well to remember that the fight for free education, equality of rights in education, etc., was probably made as a part of the movement for social recognition and equity of opportunity in the cultural and professional phases of life. To gain such concessions for all classes it was thought necessary to have the determination of school policies in the hands of the populace. But with mass education accepted by the great majority, and the problem of handing down the social inheritance, both skills and information, from generation to generation placed in the hands of the school,[24] is it not likely that the time for such purely democratic and small group control is now passed, so that, perhaps, even school policy should be formulated by professionally trained workers, rather than by a majority vote of the public?

CHAPTER III

HOW DISTRICTS COME INTO BEING—THEIR LEGAL NATURE AND THEIR AGENT BOARDS

LEGISLATURES HAVE TWO PRINCIPAL WAYS OF CREATING CITY SCHOOL DISTRICTS AND CITY BOARDS OF EDUCATION

The state legislatures have employed two principal ways of creating city school districts and city school boards.

1. One of these is by special enactment. Such enactment is usually a part of the city's charter. A city charter is a legal enactment which was at first introduced as a bill in one of the branches, or perhaps simultaneously in both branches of the state legislature, was duly considered, passed, and, if so required, signed by the governor of the state. This, then, is a special, or in a way a private act or law. It is based on the same legal principles as a private bill of any other description, such as a private pension bill, or a bill creating a commercial franchise. Among other provisions, a city charter may contain the necessary enactments to establish and maintain school districts, and provide boards of education as agents of such districts.

2. The other method of creating city districts is to prescribe certain rules and regulations to which any city eligible must conform to be allowed the rights and privileges of autonomy in the matter of its public schools. The principal conditions prescribed as essentials in practically all states which so provide for independent districts are:

a. The size of the city must be such as to entitle it to so act; and, in many states the size will also be a basis for classifications determining more accurately the powers and duties of the district and of its board.

b. There must be appointed or elected a board of education, meeting the legal specifications as to size, and other qualifications, to control the schools.

c. The board as agent of the district must conform to the letter of the law in all specified powers, not exceed the absolute implications of all implied powers, and abstain from exercising specifically or impliedly denied powers.

d. Districts and boards are almost universally declared by the statutes of the several states to be "bodies corporate." But in reality they have but *quasi* corporate powers, and they are never "bodies politic," even though some statutes do so declare them to be. They have only limited powers of a corporation and are never a governing body of any political unit.

POWERS GENERALLY DELEGATED TO BOARDS OF EDUCATION BY STATUTES

In those states where city boards are created by the general law, and in many cases where they come into existence through special law or charter provision, they are endowed with the power to sue and be sued. Likewise, they are often declared or implied to be "bodies corporate." But as before noted, they are, strictly speaking, *quasi* corporations; and as such, they have perpetuity of existence. They belong to that class of corporations that are known as "civil corporations." They are "near-public," rather than private, civil corporations, because they are for the government and management of public affairs. They are non-stock corporations, and as *quasi* corporations, they have some, but not all, of the powers of a corporation.

THE LEGAL NATURE OF A CORPORATION

"A corporation aggregate is a collection of individuals united, by authority of law, into one body, under a special denomination, *with the capacity of continuous succession,* and of acting in many respects as an individual."[1] Every corporation aggregate consists of:

1. A collection of individuals.[2]
2. A legal entity, which is, for many purposes, in contemplation of law, separate and distinct from the members who compose it.[3]

For the purpose of acquiring, holding and conveying property, contracting obligations, incurring liabilities, suing and being sued, a corporation is regarded in law as a legal entity, separate and distinct from the members who compose it. For instance:

1. The property of a corporation is owned by the corporation, and not by the individual members.[4]
2. Conveyance of such property must be made by the corporation, and cannot be made by the members as individuals.[5] This is the legal reason for insisting that a board of education act as a unit and never as individuals.
3. Suits on causes of action accruing in favor or against a corporation must be brought by or against the corporation, and not by or against the members as individuals.[6]
4. A corporation may take from and convey to its members, and may contract with them, and may sue them and be sued by them.[7] But with the board of education which is a *quasi* corporation, this right to contract with its own members is against public policy,[8] and is most often expressly prohibited in the school codes; and, where it is not so prohibited, the courts will so hold it, unless it is expressly stated in the law that such contracts shall be legal. In such cases the law always hedges these liabilities with great restrictions.

"That a corporation is thus a legal entity, separate and distinct from the members who compose it, is a mere legal fiction, introduced for the convenience of the corporation in transacting business, and of those who do business with it; and, when urged to an intent and purpose not within its reason and policy, the fiction will be disregarded, and the fact that the corporation is really a collection of individuals will be recognized in equity, and even at law."[9]

A corporation can be created only by or with the consent and authority of the state, and never by mere agreement between or among the members. This authority is given only by the state legislature.[10] Created in this way, it has such powers only as are conferred upon it, expressly or impliedly, by the charter, special act, or by the general act by which it has become incorporated. The implied powers may be of two kinds:

1. Those that are implied because they are necessary to any corporate existence.[11]
2. Those implied because they are of necessity required in order to exercise the powers expressly conferred upon the corporation.[12]

A corporation has all of the powers expressly conferred upon it unless such express powers are in violation of constitutional or treaty limitations.

As a *quasi* corporation, a board of education has the following rights and powers, which, because they are all, and the only ones that are, absolutely essential for the board's corporate existence, may be said to be inherent in the board:

1. Continuity of succession, as an artificial person under a certain name, not subject to dissolution, change of name or of its identity by the withdrawal, ejection, legal disability or death of individual members.[13]
2. To enjoy as a board immunities and grants of privileges from the legislature.[14]
3. To hold and convey property, to make contractual obligations within the limits of its charter, general statutes or grants; and to sue and be sued as a corporate individual.[15]

In giving the decision in the Dartmouth College Case, Chief Justice John Marshall said: "A corporation is an artificial being, invisible, intangible, and existing only in contemplation of the law. Being the mere creature of the law, it possesses only those properties which the charter of its creation confers upon it, either expressly, or incidental to its very existence. These are such as are supposedly best calculated to effect the object for which it was created. Among the most important are perpetuity, and, if the expression may be allowed, individuality; properties by which a perpetual succession of many persons are considered as the same, and may act as a single individual. They enable a corporation to manage its own affairs, and to hold property without the perplexing intricacies, the hazardous and endless necessity, of perpetual conveyances for the purpose of transmitting it from hand to hand. It is chiefly for the purpose of clothing bodies of men in succession with these qualities and capacities that corporations were invented, and are used. By these means, a perpetual succession of individuals is capable of acting for the promotion of a particular object, like one immortal being."

As a *quasi* corporation, then, a board of education has:

1. Perpetual succession, or perpetuity.
2. Rights and powers expressly granted by the legislature, which are not unconstitutional, or in violation of treaties.
3. Necessarily implied powers for the fulfillment of its express purpose.[16]

CHAPTER IV

BOARDS OF EDUCATION: PRESENT LEGAL STATUS

DEFINITIONS

"A city school board is a board of officers charged with the administration of the affairs of the public schools. They are commonly organized under the general laws of the state, and fall within the class of *quasi* corporations, sometimes coterminous with the city, county or borough, but not necessarily so. The members of the board are sometimes called 'school directors', or the official style may be 'the board of school directors'. The circuit of their territorial jurisdiction is called 'a school district,' and each school district is usually a separate taxing district for school purposes."[1] Other appellations sometimes used to designate a city school board are: "The Board of Education"; "The School Board"; "The School Committee"; "School Trustees"; "The Board of School Trustees"; "School Commissioners"; and perhaps others are used less frequently and in a few scattered communities.

THREE KINDS OF SCHOOL BOARDS

In the eyes of the law, school boards are of three kinds when viewed from the standpoint of the source and legality of their authority. They are:

1. *De facto* boards.
2. *De jure* boards.
3. Usurpers, or intruders.

1. *De Facto* Boards:

The *de facto* board is one which is not legally elected and qualified, but, nevertheless, its acts will stand as legal in so far as they are reasonably calculated to promote the best interests of the district and its school system. In other words, a *de facto* member of the board, or a *de facto* board, is one which is in actual possession of the office and is actively engaged in administering the official duties and functions of the office but has not the lawful title to hold or so administer the offices.

2. *De Jure* Boards:

On the other hand, a *de jure* member of a board, or a *de jure* board, is one which has the lawful title to the office, regardless of who is in actual possession of it. That is to say, that a *de jure* member or board is one who should be in legal possession of, but is prevented by circumstances from administering, the office in question.

3. Usurpers or Intruders:

Usurpers or intruders, either as individuals or as a board, have no legal standing whatsoever. Their acts are void *ab initio:* and cannot be legal or enforceable against a district unless later ratified by a board or some one having legal capacity to bind the district. However, innocent parties may recover from usurpers as individuals, any losses sustained as a result of the false pretensions of the usurper.

THE BOARD AN AGENT OF THE STATE LEGISLATURE

As has been said in a previous chapter, a city board of education is an agent of the district, and, since the district is but an agent of the state, it follows that the city board is an indirect or subagent of the state, and as such is answerable in many ways directly to its principal, the state. Both the district and the board have been created either by the general law, the city charter, or by special enactment of the state legislature. Consequently, these agents derive from the legislature all of their just powers, as they are set forth and defined in the constitutional acts of the legislature. Neither the district nor the board can lawfully perform any acts or enjoy any powers which have not been so set forth and defined in the charter or the statutes, or have not been absolutely implied by them. And should the district or the board, either through ignorance of the law or intentionally, perform any acts or exercise any powers, not so specified or necessarily and absolutely implied, such acts will be held by the courts to be *ultra vires,* or beyond the pale of the authority of the agent so acting.[2]

BOARD MEMBERS PUBLIC OFFICERS OF THE STATE

The nature of the city board's authority is that of public officers to whom has been given definite authority in school matters, while at the same time they are charged with and are absolutely answerable for corresponding responsibilities. Nor can either powers or these obligations be usurped by the district; and, in case the district attempt such subversion, the courts will hold that the board has very large discretionary powers, extending even to refusal to carry out directions voted by the district when such directions impinge upon the board's proper business.[3]

CRITERIA FOR DETERMINING WHAT IS A PUBLIC OFFICER

As public officials, the powers and duties of the city school board must fulfill the requisites of the following criteria of a public office:

1. There must be a certain amount of delegated sovereign power.
2. Oath of office, or other definite acts of qualifying for the office.
3. The giving of bond, or other pledging of personal liability.
4. There must be definite tenure of office.

These criteria have been definitely fixed in general by the state courts of Ohio [4] and Wisconsin,[5] and by the United States Federal courts.[6] They were emphasized with special reference to school officers in the case of Sickle v. People tried in the city of Baltimore, July, 1910.[7] From these cases the courts will hold that the powers and duties implied by these criteria are inherent in boards of education for the reason that they are public officials and these powers are inherent in all public officials.

HOW A BOARD OF EDUCATION COMES INTO EXISTENCE

Subsequent to the time that the legislature provides the legal machinery for a city board to come into being, either through the general law by which municipal districts are organized, through the city charter, or by special enactment, a board, such as is specified by the legislature, is selected either by election or by appointment according to whichever method has been indicated by the legislature, the selection being made by the electorate, either limited or unlimited, or it is made by some municipal or civic power to whom the legislature has delegated the proper authority. The relative number of states in which these several methods are practiced is set forth in a preceding chapter.

It is commonly accepted by careful students of this question that it is the better practice to have the city boards selected by the electorate at a special school election. This prevents the school issues from being overshadowed or confused with the municipal, state or national issues, as would be the case if the election were held at the time of a general election. Furthermore, the elected board is free from any obligation to any political officer, or officials charged with the appointive power. It is quite generally agreed by those most prepared to judge that complete independence of this influence is desirable.

THE ACTS OF QUALIFYING: THE MEMBER

Before taking office, and after being elected, it is obligatory that each member individually qualify for his office. The procedure for qualifying is almost without exception prescribed by the several codes. In most of the states it consists in taking the oath of office, sometimes orally, while sometimes a signed oath is required to be filed with the clerk or some other official. In a few states the members must be in possession of "letters of election", certificate of election or other documentary evidence of their official capacity to be present at, and to participate in the business of, a board meeting.[8]

THE BOARD AS A WHOLE: ORGANIZATION

The board as such must further qualify by organizing and electing its own officers [9] as prescribed in the statutes. This is usually done at the first meeting, and this meeting is generally called the "annual meeting". Any other statutory directions, such as the time, place, nature of the meeting, etc., must be strictly adhered to, or the acts of the board will not be binding beyond question.

QUALIFICATIONS FOR MEMBERSHIP ON CITY BOARDS OF EDUCATION

The personnel of the board is, without exception, composed of residents of the district for which the board is selected. Where the board is elected, the right to exercise the franchise is always a condition to membership on the board. But where the board is appointed, this would not be true, and in the latter case, even citizenship would not necessarily be a prerequisite, or the lack of it a bar to membership. In some states, a greater age than a mere majority is required but in most states twenty-one is the age necessary for eligibility.[10] The same age is always required of both sexes.

Since the universal enfranchisement of women in 1918 by the Nineteenth Amendment to the Federal Constitution, women are eligible equally with men to membership on all school boards. Prior to the adoption of this amendment, women were eligible both as electors of and as members of city boards of education in a majority of the states. In a few states they were given suffrage in all matters by constitutional provision, either by the original constitutions or by amendments thereto. But in the majority of states women were made special electors for the election of school board members by legislative enactment, because, to do this required only the passage of a bill, while to have given them the vote for state officials would have required revision or amendment of the constitution. This was difficult to do and was accomplished in but a few cases, because it was quite generally thought that given the vote, women would quickly cause to be enacted prohibition of the manufacture and sale of intoxicants and would also secure the passage of other anti-vice legislation. Consequently, these powers of privilege united to prevent what otherwise would long since have come to pass, viz., the equality of political rights so far as sexes were concerned.

In a small minority of the states ownership of property, usually a small amount, is one of the qualifications for either voting or being eligible to board membership, or both. Whatever tendency there has been in the last quarter century, it has been away from this practice of requiring property rights as necessary to voting or board membership.

Parentage, or, *loco parentis,*—standing in the relationship of a parent,—is occasionally a prerequisite to voting for or acting as school officials. This practice, too, is becoming more infrequent as the spirit of democracy gains impetus throughout our whole system of government and throughout our institutions.

Other less common qualifications are found now and then. "Literally, a proper person," "a sober person," and others could be cited. As a rule, however, all persons who have not been officially judged as *non compos mentis* may vote for, or hold board memberships, provided that they are of legal age and can secure appointment or election according to whichever system of selection happens to prevail.

CHAPTER V

PRINCIPLES OF CODE DEVELOPMENT

STATEMENT IN OUTLINE OF THE PRINCIPLES UNDERLYING CODE MAKING

In attempting to formulate the principles which underlie the making or drafting of school codes it seems best to approach the problem as outlined below. It should be clearly in mind, above all else, that these principles are not here being "created"; and that they are not just now being "discovered." The fact is that these principles are all as old as school law itself, to say nothing of the fact that many of them are as old as law itself. What is really being done is the twofold task of collecting these principles, both those that have been formally stated, and those which have been merely "working principles," but never stated in written form, or at best but poorly and inadequately stated; and of stating them in organized and concise form. The outline follows:

A. Definitions of Law.
   1. Definitions and purposes.
   2. Criteria for all law.

B. School Law.
   1. Historical.
   2. Special aspects of good school law.
   3. Criteria for good school law.
   4. Form and content of school law.

C. Principles underlying the criteria for the selection and statement of school law.

DEFINITIONS

"Law is a system of principles and rules of human conduct, being the aggregate of those commandments and principles which are either prescribed or recognized by the governing power in an organized jural society as its will in relation to the conduct of the members of such society, and which it undertakes to maintain and sanction and to use as the criteria of the actions of such members."[1]

"Municipal law is properly defined to be a rule of civil conduct prescribed by the supreme power in a state, commanding what is right and prohibiting what is wrong."[2]

PURPOSES OF LEGAL PRINCIPLES

"For when civil society is once formed, government at the same time results of course, as necessary to preserve and keep that society in order. Unless some superior be constituted, whose commands and decisions all the members are bound to obey, they would still remain as in a state of nature, without any judge upon earth to define their several rights, and redress their several wrongs. But as all the members which compose this society were naturally equal, it may be asked, in whose hands are the reins of government to be entrusted? To this the general answer is easy; but the application of it to particular cases has occasioned one half of those mischiefs which are apt to proceed from misguided political zeal. In general, all mankind will agree that government should be reposed in such persons in whom those qualities are most likely to be found, the perfection of which is among the attributes of Him who is emphatically styled the Supreme Being; the three grand requisites, I mean, of wisdom, of goodness, and of power; wisdom to discern the real interests of the community; goodness to endeavor always to pursue that real interest; and strength or power to carry this knowledge and intention into action. These are the natural foundations of sovereignty, and these are the requisites that ought to be found in every well constituted frame of government."[3]

CRITERIA FOR ALL LAW

The practices which are enacted into law should always be consistent with certain underlying, fundamental principles, among which are the following:

1. The practice should be greatly comprehensive, that is, very inclusive. For example, Blackstone says, that to ancient British

laws were added many of the Roman customs, the Picts, the Saxons, the Danes and the Normans, "thereby, in all probability, improving the texture and wisdom of the whole by the accumulated wisdom of diverse particular countries." [4]

2. Other things being equal, long usage or *stare decisis* will indicate intrinsic value in a law. This is on the assumption that it will have undergone those processes of evolution generally implied by the term, "the survival of the fittest." In this connection, Blackstone says: it must have been used so long that, "the mind of man runneth not to the contrary."

3. Generally speaking, the practice should have been continuous, and not just followed intermittently. The latter practice will indicate one of several conditions among which are:

a. Uncertainty of the soundness of the practice.
b. Attempts to remedy temporary conditions by general legislation.
c. A division of the people into about equal groups, one group favoring the legislation, the other opposed to it.
d. The work of propagandists securing from time to time spasmodic practice under emotional stimuli.

4. The practice should be one that has been peaceably agreed to. Unless this is true, the particular practice may represent the work of a tyrannical majority, or even the usurpations of a minority.

5. The practice should be reasonably consistent with the spirit of the law. Unless it is so, the courts will certainly abrogate the law as unconstitutional, against public policy, or *ultra vires,* etc.

6. The practice must be certain, not indefinite or obscured in meaning or necessary implications.

7. In common law, the practice must have been compulsory. This is not necessary as a criterion for statutory law, but whenever it has been true, it will be a positive and absolute criterion.

8. The practice must be consistent with other legal principles. A legal system which would attempt to apply specific principles in disregard of other principles would be utterly impotent, unstable and certain of destruction.

9. The law or statute itself should be properly constructed.

"For this purpose every law may be said to consist of several parts; one 'declaratory'; whereby the rights to be observed, and the wrongs to be eschewed, are clearly defined and laid down; another, 'directory,' whereby the subject is instructed and enjoined to observe those rights, and to abstain from the commission of those wrongs; a third, 'remedial,' whereby a method is pointed out for adjusting rights and redressing wrongs. To these may be added a fourth, usually termed the 'sanction,' or vindicatory branch of the law; whereby it is signified what evil or penalty shall be incurred by such as commit any public wrongs, and transgress or neglect their duty." [5]

IMPORTANT MILESTONES IN THE DEVELOPMENT OF LEGAL PRINCIPLES PERTAINING TO EDUCATION

1. *Ancient Legal Provisions.* As long ago as the days of ancient Greece, the moral obligation of the parent to educate the child was pointed out by Solon, the Lawgiver of Athens, in his adjudication of cases growing out of personal relations arising from the failure of Athenian youths to assume the care of their aged parents. "For this purpose he made a law, that no son should be obliged to maintain his father, if he had not taught him a trade." [6]

2. *Common Law Obligations of Parent to Child.* The oldest pronouncements of the English legal system on education are those to be found in the Common Law. Tiffany in discussing these, says: "It is sometimes said by text-writers that it is the duty of a parent to give his children an education suitable to their station in life,[7] and there are dicta in many cases to the same effect.[8] This duty, however, is only a moral one. There is no legal duty on the part of a parent to educate his children, however wealthy he may be. At least, there seems to be no case in which such a duty has been enforced, either directly or indirectly. Education is not necessary to the subsistence of a child, and the reasons which should, and in some states do, render a parent legally bound to support his child do not apply." [9]

3. *Common Law Obligation of a Guardian to His Ward.* In the matter of guardian and ward, it was doubtless felt that, the natural parental affection being absent, the ward's rights and

interests might be impaired in some way for the fiduciary benefit of the guardian. To guard against this, the Common Law is much more positive in defining the obligations of the guardian to the ward than it is in the case of parent to the child. Tiffany says: "It is the duty of the guardian to maintain and educate his ward in a manner suitable to his means, from the income of the ward's estate.[10] Although the ward's father is living, the guardian should provide for his maintenance out of his estate, provided the father is unable to do so, and a court of equity will order an allowance for such maintenance."[11]

"A guardian is under no personal obligation to support his ward, and therefore no promise on his part will be implied, as a matter of law, to pay even for his ward's necessaries. 'A guardian is not responsible, either personally or in his fiduciary character, for necessaries furnished his ward without his consent, express or implied!' "[12]

4. *Early English Statutes Bearing on Education.* The motive for the beginning of English statute law on education is found in the conditions pertaining to the apprenticeship system. The gilds had inaugurated this system to serve their own interests. The Statute of Apprentices (1562) legalized the practices and customs of the gild system. At first the contracts of apprenticeship were wholly voluntary, and being for the most part between parties of equal social station and for mutual benefit, they were productive of very satisfactory results.

The Tudor statesmen, seeing the success of this system, seized upon it as a means of combating pauperism and idleness. They secured the passage of the Statute of Artificers; and an act of 1601, entitled: "An Acte for Releife of the Poore," 43 Eliz. C. 2. The last named act made it compulsory that dependent orphans and children of indigent poor should be bound out as apprentices so that they might be taught a trade.

The apprenticeship system is of comparatively recent origin, beginning as it did with the gild system of the middle ages. "Apprenticeships were altogether unknown to the ancients. Roman Law is perfectly silent in regard to them. I know no Greek or Latin word (I might venture, I believe, to assert that there is none) which expresses the idea we now annex to the word apprentice."[13]

"The gild system with its handicraft methods, its production solely for local markets, its steady employment, uniform wages, and lack of business depressions and panics, makes an ideal setting for a very complete and thorough system of apprenticeship. The youth was bound out, or indentured by his parents to a master with whom he lived and in whose shop the trade was learned, the master agreeing to furnish the apprentice with food, clothing and shelter and to teach him the trade, the latter agreeing to obey the orders of the master, keep all business affairs secret; and behave himself properly under all conditions. In England the usual period of apprenticeship was about 7 years; in France, from 3 and 4 years to 6; and in Germany from 2 to 4 years, after which the apprentice became a journeyman with all the rights and privileges of the latter.

"The Statute of Apprentices (1562) legalized the practices and customs of the gild system. It declared that no one could engage in any trade without having served as an apprentice for 7 years."[14] It fixed the number of apprentices at 3 for each journeyman employed, set the hours of labor, and directed that the magistrates fix, from time to time, the wages.

The act of 1601 brought to a culmination a series of provisions in various statutes, viz., 27 Hen. VIII. C. 25; 1 Edw. VI. C. 3; 5 Eliz. C. 4; 39 Eliz. C. 3; and 43 Eliz. C. 2, relating to compulsory apprenticeship of poor children who otherwise would have been burdens to the state. The fifth section of the acts says: "It shall be lawful for the said church wardens and the overseers (of the poor) or the greater part of them, by the assent of any two justices of the peace aforesaid, to bind any such children, as aforesaid, to be apprentices, where they shall see convenient, till such man-child shall come to the age of four and twenty years, and such woman-child to the age of one and twenty years, or the time of her marriage."

The contracts made under these statutes remained subject to the rules of the Common Law on guardian and ward so far as a literary education was concerned. That is, if the apprentice had an estate which would permit, the master must provide such education; or, if the master agreed in contract to furnish such education he would be legally bound to do so and the courts would compel performance. "No general law to compel masters to see to education (other than instruction in a craft) of parish apprentices was enacted in England, however, until 1802."[15]

5. *Colonial Educational Laws.* The obligations of parents and of those *in loco parentis* to the child, both express and implied, by the Common Law and by the statutes of England extant at the time, were part of the legal heritage of our colonial ancestors. Couple this fact with the Puritans' desire that each person be able to read the Bible, and it is not surprising to find them passing regulatory provisions in the matter of education 22 years after the arrival of the *Mayflower;* and a rather comprehensive set of school enactments 5 years later, in 1647.

In discussing the status of education at Plymouth prior to 1642, Cubberley says: "As in England, the system was voluntary, and clearly subordinate to the church. It early became evident, however, that these voluntary efforts on the part of the people and the towns would not be sufficient to insure that general education which was required by the Puritan religious theory. Under the hard pioneer conditions and the suffering which ensued, many parents and masters of apprentices apparently proved neglectful of their educational duties. Accordingly the leaders of the Puritan Church appealed to what was then their servant, the State as represented in the colonial legislature, to assist them in compelling parents and masters to observe their obligations. The result was the famous Massachusetts Law of 1642, which directed the officials of each town to ascertain, from time to time, if parents and masters were attending to their educational duties; if all children were being trained "in learning and labor and other employments profitable to the Commonwealth"; and if children were being taught "to read and understand the principles of religion and the capital laws of the country." The officers were empowered to impose fines on those who failed to give proper instruction, or to report to the officer when required. This law of 1642 is remarkable in that, for the first time in the English-speaking world, a legislative body representing the State ordered that all children should be taught to read.[16]

"The law (1642), however, did not establish schools, nor did it direct the employment of school masters. After true English fashion, the provision of education was still left with the homes. The results still continuing unsatisfactory, five years later the colonial legislature enacted the famous Law of 1647, by means of which it has been asserted that, 'the Puritan government of

Massachusetts rendered its greatest service to the future.' The Law then ordered:

"*a.* That every town having 50 householders should at once appoint a teacher of reading and writing, and provide for his wages in such manner as the town might determine; and

"*b.* That every town having 100 householders must provide a (Latin) grammar school to fit youths for the university, under a penalty of £5 for failure to do so.

"This Law represents a distinct advance over the Law of 1642. The State here, acting again as the servant of the Church, enacted a Law for which there were no English precedents. Not only was a school system ordered established—elementary for all towns and children, and secondary for the youths in the larger towns—but, for the first time among English-speaking people, there was the assertion of the right of the State to require communities to establish and maintain schools, under penalty of a fine if they refused to do so." [17]

The Massachusetts Laws soon became prototypes for similar laws enacted in all of the remaining New England colonies except Rhode Island. In the middle colonies the doctrine of *laissez-faire* most nearly represents the status of educational law concerning non-orphan children, while the apprentice system applied to orphan and indigent poor during the whole of the Colonial Period. Intermittent attempts were made to establish state schools, but they met with little or indifferent success.[18]

In the southern colonies the apprentice system was early adopted as is evidenced by the apprenticeship laws of Virginia under the dates of 1643, 1646 and 1672; and of North Carolina court records of 1695, 1703 and 1713.[19] Under this system the Common Law principle, that the guardian must educate the ward according to the competence of the ward's estate, held. "It was not until 1705 that Virginia reached the point reached by Massachusetts in 1642 of requiring that 'the master of the (apprenticed) orphan shall be obliged to teach him to read and write.' " [20]

Throughout this transition period which lasted until after the Revolutionary War, the established churches gradually lost their control over education while the cause of public education became more hopeful. It is true that during the actual war and the readjustment period following education throughout the colonies approached very near to the vanishing point. But with the coming of independence and citizenship rights under the new government, the motive for education became political and thus completed the transition from the religious motive.

6. *A Period of Acceleration.* After the Revolutionary War the participation of the State in educational affairs grew into a pronounced movement which was destined to make educational opportunity universal and compulsory. This movement has its beginnings in the work of Thomas Jefferson. During the War Jefferson, who had been reëlected to Congress on June 20, 1776, declined the honor to accept election to the House of Delegates in Virginia. On October 7, 1776, he took his seat and was at once placed on many important committees. He began a valiant fight for personal liberty and equality of rights. Among others, he introduced a bill in the House of Delegates 1779, which provided for universal education. This bill failed to be enacted into law, but it and a later bill introduced by Jefferson in the State legislature, 1799, reflect his idea that control of the schools should be kept very closely in the hands of the people. This movement was destined to localize in extreme degree the support and control of schools, making it difficult at a later date and under changed conditions to secure sufficient centralization for economic and efficient administration of schools. This readjustment is not yet complete, and is one of the most perplexing educational problems before the state legislatures of today.[21]

In the last mentioned bill, that of 1799 which also failed of enactment, was a comprehensive scheme whereby a complete system of education was proposed for the State of Virginia. The plan was to divide each county into small districts, five or six miles square, each to be called an "Hundred" and in each of them to establish a school to teach reading, writing and arithmetic. These schools were to be open free to all children of citizens for three years, and for a longer time upon payment of tuition. From the best pupils the "visitors" were to select students to be sent to the Grammar Schools, also proposed to be established by the bill, and given further instruction. A final selection was to be made whereby the most promising were to be sent to William and Mary College.

These attempts of Jefferson were prophetic indications of what was to come in the matter of education.

7. *Constitutions.* The Articles of Confederation are silent as to education.

In the Constitution of the United States there is no direct mention of education. But as it is not among, "The powers not delegated to The United States by the Constitution, nor prohibited by it to the States," it is by the tenth amendment, "reserved to the states respectively, or to the people."

During and after the Revolutionary War some of the several states revised their Colonial Charters so that they would serve as State Constitutions under the new Union. The others made new Constitutions. In all, there were 16 states in the Federal Union by the year 1800. In the Constitutions of 9 of these 16, no mention of education was made.

But today all of the state constitutions direct their respective legislatures to provide and maintain an adequate educational system by law.[22] Acting under power of these directions, every state has provided by due legal enactment, a system of public schools. All forty-eight of the states have gone so far as to make education compulsory by law. However, in all states, attendance at private schools may be substituted for attendance in the state system.

8. *Special Aspects of American School Law.* As just seen, the age of the American school law is practically coëxtensive with the age of the first permanent settlements. It is quite distinctly American, having no exact counterpart in other nations, and in a way it has reflected American ideals of education. It is decidedly a product of trial and error method.

The variability, however, is very great. Because there is no counterpart, no definite and well tried standards, each state, and often each city, formulated new laws and legal provisions. Naturally, these new systems were fundamentally affected by the laws and usages of other states and cities, whence the new settlers came. Out of this grew 48 independent systems, varying in very great detail, as is shown by the tables of laws and frequencies in the next chapter. Yet, in spirit, all 48 of these independent systems are very much alike so that it is highly improbable that greater uniformity would lessen the effectiveness of the legal provisions pertaining to education.

CRITERIA FOR SCHOOL LAW

1. Those criteria cited on a preceding page as of all law will *a priori* be essential criteria for school laws.
2. Authority and responsibility must be adequate to guarantee the best possible school system commensurate with the funds available.
3. Certainty of statement and interpretation.
4. Simplicity of form and organization.
5. Practicability.
6. Adaptable for general application throughout the state.

RECENT AND PRESENT TRENDS

"Each of the 48 states has its own distinct system of education. The Federal Government assumes no control over the public schools throughout the country except with reference to the special Federal appropriations for specific purposes, as the Smith-Hughes Act for assistance to vocational education and the Smith-Lever Act for assistance to agricultural extension education. Nevertheless, because of proximity and interchange of ideas, the State systems have many points of similarity. Conditions affecting the kinds of school systems do not differ fundamentally; therefore, each State profits by the experiences of others, and through the adoption of what proves good the States are tending toward systems more similar than in the past. We have, therefore, what may be designated as the 'trend in school law-development' in the United States, an expression meaning the forward movement—generally toward similarity in systems and practices." [23]

LEGISLATURES GUIDED BY THE EXPERIENCE OF OTHER STATES

In enacting school laws, legislatures may be guided in part by the experiences of other States. For instance, in one state some one recommends legislation to provide that the state prepare and print its own textbooks. Before final action is taken the experiences of California and Kansas may well be studied. Another proposes the adoption of the county unit of administration and support; a study of the experiences of states organized on that basis will be helpful. When it is evident that new or revised school laws are needed in any state, it is wise to follow the successful experiences of other states which have tried the proposed plans, if such may be found. If reasons are evident that would make this practice undesirable, or a plan is proposed which seems better than any yet tried, a review of the experiences of other states solving the same problems in other ways is still desirable.

In other words, school legislation should be passed in the light of what has been proved effective in other states and with the knowledge before the legislators of what has been tried and discarded; and of the reasons influencing such success or failure.[24]

"In the preparation of a law to govern the local management of the schools of our cities, sound business principles and pedagogical standards must be respected to the end that our city schools shall meet more completely and efficiently the constantly increasing demands which are made upon them. The following fundamental principles must be observed:

1. "The absolute divorcement of the school affairs from the other municipal and political activities of the city.
2. "The professional direction of the school system should be under the charge of the superintendent of schools. This should include the right to nominate assistant superintendents, supervisors, directors and teachers, and to determine the qualifications of teachers, courses of study, etc.
3. "The purely business administrative features of the system should be under the management and direction of the board of education.
4. "Boards of estimate and apportionment of common councils should be required to include in the tax budget annually a specified minimum amount for the maintenance of the schools. They should have discretion to include a greater sum.
5. "The funds set apart for the schools should be under the direct control of the board of education and should be expended on the order of the board only.
6. "The sites selected for buildings and the plans and specifications for repairs or additions to present buildings or the

construction of new buildings should require the approval of the board of education.

7. "The board of education must be composed of a sufficient number to make it a strong, representative, workable body. It should not be so small in numbers that one or two may dominate its action. It should not be so large in numbers as to make it cumbersome and unwieldly. A board of seven members is suggested.
8. "The method of electing the members of a board of education is important. Members should not be chosen at a general election. When members are so chosen, the interests of the school are involved in the political issues of the city and men are often chosen upon the determination of the political issues involved instead of their special fitness to serve in such a capacity. The best men in a city will often decline to allow their names to be used at a popular election involving municipal politics when they would willingly accept an appointment from the mayor and render the schools of their city valuable services. In a community desiring the members to be chosen directly by the people, the election should be a separate school election and not at the same time as the municipal election. The method of selecting members of a board of education therefore should be either by appointment by the mayor or by election by the people at a date specifically set for such election."[25]

ORIGIN OF POLITICAL POWERS AND THE AGENCIES THROUGH WHICH THEY PASS

The original source from which all school codes, as well as all other codes, derive their just powers is the people of the nation. The agencies through which all such political power passes in order to effect their ultimate purposes, namely, the education of the youth of the land, are depicted by the accompanying diagram.

From this diagram, it is seen that the original source is in the people of the nation, who, by neither appropriating this power for the Federal Government nor denying it to the several states, reserved it to the people of each state, who in turn, through their

DIAGRAM I

SHOWING THE SOURCE OF POWER TO CREATE AND MAINTAIN SCHOOLS, AND THE AGENCIES THROUGH WHICH THAT POWER PASSES TO THE PUPILS CONTROLLED

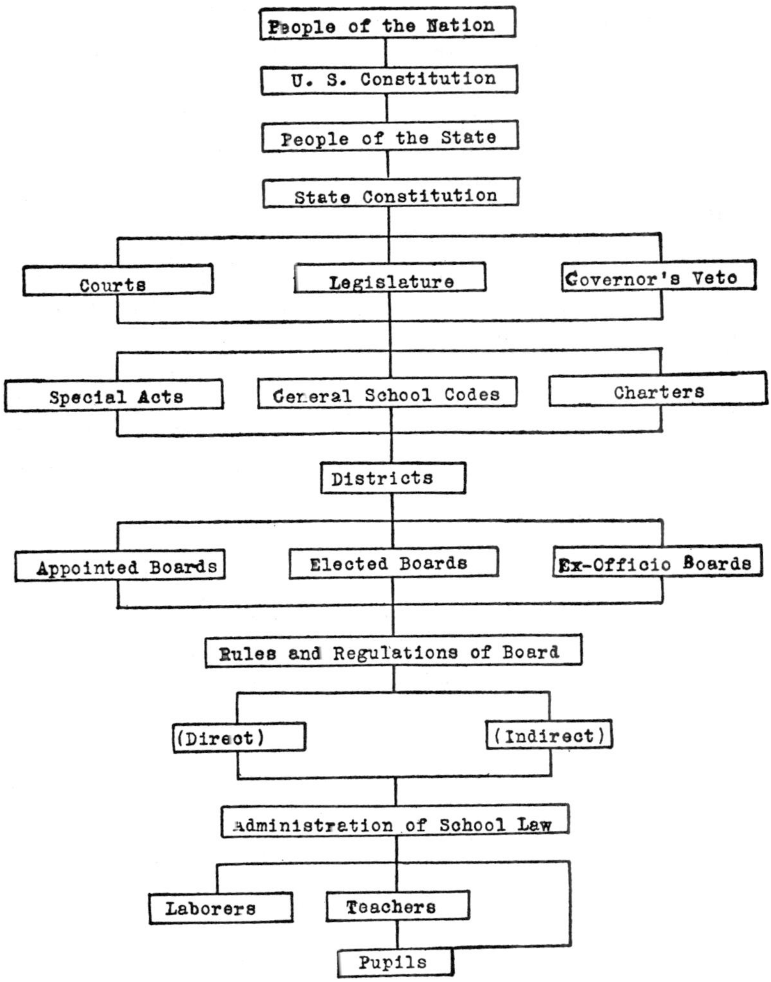

state constitutions, delegated it to their respective legislatures, with the customary limiting powers of the courts and of the governor's advice (through his message) and his veto power where he enjoys this function. The legislatures, in turn, without exception have further delegated the actual control of the school through legislative enactment to local agencies, either directly or indirectly, i. e., through general law or through charters. These local agencies, universally, or almost universally, called districts, have in varying degree still further delegated these powers to lawfully constituted boards, variously selected, sometimes appointed, sometimes elected, and sometimes functioning ex-officio. Examples: City of Buffalo; also, formerly, St. Paul. These local boards or managers are empowered as a rule, to draft certain rules and regulations for their own government as a board, and for the government of the schools; and, in so far as these rules and regulations are not inconsistent with the provisions of the laws set forth by any higher authority, they are, to all intents and purposes, *bona fide* law; and they, together with the statutory law, must be observed by all who have any part in the actual administration or operation of the schools of the state.

THE ADMINISTRATION OF SCHOOL LAW

The law and the rules and regulations of the board are then administered in two principal ways, viz., directly and indirectly. The indirect, or at least partially indirect and usually more indirect than direct, is almost the universal method. By this method the actual administration of the legal provisions is left to designated executives of the board, such as superintendent of schools, the president of the board, the secretary of the board, committees of the board, etc. But under either direct or indirect method, the work of educating the young is finally accomplished through the teaching corps of the school, assisted by diverse nonteaching employees, such as janitors, engineers, etc., designated in the chart as "labor".

FINAL OBJECTIVES OF SCHOOL LAW

The ultimate objective of the foregoing scheme of educational law is obviously three-fold, viz:

1. To establish and maintain a policy of education which will be adequate for all of the children of the given state.
2. To create efficient machinery for the administration of an all inclusive system of schools.
3. To reserve in the hands of the state the power to amend and change both the policy and the administrative organization from time to time, thereby guarding against it becoming formal or static.

CHAPTER VI

POWERS AND DUTIES OF CITY SCHOOL BOARDS AS INDICATED IN STATE STATUTES

PURPOSE OF THIS CHAPTER

When once a duly authorized and properly selected board has fully qualified and organized according to law, it is then in proper status to function, as the agent of the district and of the state in its purported task of operating the schools of the district. In this capacity the city boards of the United States have a great variety of powers and duties, and these aspects of the city board problem now become the focus of investigation.

To determine the range of the powers which the statutes of the several states specifically grant to city boards and to secure the frequency of occurrence of these powers, it was necessary to analyze the school codes of the forty-eight states, which were in effect during each of the years for which a cross section study was desired. These analyses for the years 1901, 1911 and 1921 are described in some detail in the following pages.*

METHOD OF ANALYSIS

The method used to make the analysis of the codes of the forty-eight states for each of the three years 1901, 1911 and 1921 was as follows:

1. The school codes which were in effect during each of these three years were secured. These could not be obtained directly from the respective states as many of them were out of print, and the different institutions and departments of the several states either did not have them in file or else refused to loan them by mail, offering as reasons that they had but one copy; that their copies were needed locally; that loaning outside of their

* The table containing the original data mentioned in this chapter is bound in duplicate and filed in the library of Teachers College, Columbia University.

immediate state or clientele was against the rules and regulations of the institutions; etc. Consequently, a month spent in the Congressional Library where the codes of all the states along with other important state documents have been deposited, yielded the necessary data.

2. Each code was carefully read and the powers and duties of city boards transcribed in the order in which they occurred in the laws. This method was necessary because there is absolutely no uniformity, either in the order in which these functions are stated or in the form of the statements. And, of course, no comprehensive list of these powers could be compiled prior to the analysis of the codes. Could this have been done, a checking system could have been used which would have greatly reduced the labor of collecting the data.

3. After the data were transcribed under the heads of the states and as of the years to which they belonged, a card system, after various attempts at other methods had proved unsatisfactory, was used. By this system a brief statement of the law was written at the top of the card, the body of the card lined off in three sections and headed respectively by 1901, 1911, and 1921. A sample of the card is inserted.

4. Next, the states were assigned their proper numbers in consecutive order as they appear in the official United States census, which is of course alphabetically, and this number was arbitrarily considered as the index number of the state to which it belonged, and so used thereafter to designate this particular state.

5. Then the transcribed laws of each state and for each of the three years were read, and, whenever a state had any given

DIAGRAM II.

SAMPLE CARD ON WHICH WAS ENTERED THE INDEX NUMBER OF THE STATES WHOSE CODES CONTAINED THE LAW STATED IN BRIEF AT THE TOP OF THE CARD

10. BLANKET CONTROL OF THE SCHOOLS		
1901	1911	1921
1, 10, 13, 14, 19, 20, 21, 23, 24, 35, 36, 37, 39, 40, 41, 42, 43, 45, 46, 47,	1, 10, 11, 13, 14, 19, 20, 23, 24, 30, 33, 36, 37, 39, 40, 41, 42, 43, 45, 46, 47, 48,	1, 7, 10, 11, 12, 14, 15, 19, 20, 24, 27, 30, 35, 36, 37, 39, 40, 41, 42, 43, 44, 45, 46, 47, 48,

law for any one of these three years, the index number for that state was entered in that section of the card devoted to the year in question. No attempt was made, even at this time, to compile a list of these laws. Instead, new cards were added only when new laws appeared in the transcribed notes. This work of preparing this card system, so briefly told, occupied, on an average, three hours per day for four months. At the end of that time the brief statements of the laws on the cards were transcribed alphabetically to tabular form, and so arranged that the index numbers of the states having each law could be entered as of the proper year. Thus was made what may be called a parent table.

6. The next step was taken as a matter of precaution, looking to the end that the data to be submitted might contain as few errors as it is humanly possible to achieve in a study dealing with material so easily misconstrued as are the statutes of any state. The step consisted of preparing data sheets with the list of brief statements of the laws arranged with tabular spaces just large enough to enter the data for any one state. The data sheets were headed with blank spaces for the name and address of the checker; and, for the name and index number of the state. The data for each state were then entered in triplicate and copies sent to the deans or heads of the leading law schools, to the deans or heads of the educational administration departments of leading teacher training colleges, and to the state departments of each of the forty-eight states. These institutions were asked to check the data for their respective states and make any necessary corrections. In the selection of the schools to which the data were sent, state institutions, other things being equal, were chosen in preference to other institutions. When these data sheets were returned from the several states they were checked with the original parent or master table. If corrections or additions had been made they were rechecked with the codes, if available, if not, then with the original digests of the codes. If the corrections and additions were found to be accurate, they were entered on the master table. This completed the work of analysis, tabulation, and checking.

7. The master table was then typewritten, using the number of the states in alphabetical order, thus, 1, 2, 3, 4, 5, 6, 7, 8, 9, 10, 1, 2, 3, 4, 5, 6, 7, 8, 9, 20, 1, 2, 3, 4, 5, 6, 7, 8, 9, 30, 1,

2, 3, 4, 5, 6, 7, 8, 9, 40, 1, 2, 3, 4, 5, 6, 7, 8, as indices for the states; and, the consecutive numbers from 1 to 204 as indices for the laws as they appear in the list of "Brief Statement of the Laws," and on which they had been entered to send out to the several state institutions to be checked.

Table III shows totals for frequencies of the briefly stated laws, prescribing city school board functions, which were found to occur throughout the 48 states. Because of the great variety of ways used in the state codes to express any given legal enactment, and of the variation in detail, often very slight, of the provisions thereof, these totals, when compared to the whole

TABLE III

DATA SHEET

POWERS AND DUTIES OF CITY SCHOOL BOARDS

No.	Brief Statement of the Laws	1901	1911	1921
1.	Academies, contract with for high school education....	1	1	2
2.	Agents, cannot be for texts, supplies, etc.	4	4	5
3.	Americanization work, provide for	..	..	5
4.	Apportion all school funds among the schools........	6	5	7
5.	Appropriate money for school purposes...............	1	2	2
6.	Arbor Day duties, plant trees, etc.....................	1	2	3
7.	Attorney, select regular or have ex-officio.............	3	5	6
8.	Bids, let contracts on, if specified amount............	7	12	13
9.	Bids, right to refuse any or all......................	1	3	4
10.	Blanket control, board has of the schools.............	21	23	24
11.	Bonds, require political officials to bond.............	1	1	2
12.	Bonds, issue when so voted	7	6	9
13.	Bonds, issue for debts within specified amount........	3	4	6
14.	Bonds, issue for building, within specified amount.....	1	3	3
15.	Bonds, reserve right to redeem before maturity........	1	1	2
16.	Bonds, required of those who handle money...........	15	15	14
17.	Bonds, specified amount for those who handle money...	5	4	3
18.	Books, financial, audit or have audited...............	8	9	8
19.	Borrow, specified amount of anticipated income.......	3	4	7
20.	Budget, estimate to some higher power...............	8	10	14
21.	Budget, must make at beginning of year.............	3	3	8
22.	Budget, must make for own use and follow...........	1	2	2
23.	Build structures when so voted......................	8	8	12
24.	Build structures at own discretion	6	11	13
25.	Code, no important changes in during 1901-21.........	2	2	3
26.	Code, provides city districts only through charters.....	5	4	3
27.	Committees, appoint all special and standing..........	2	5	6
28.	Compensation, board fixes own	2	1	2
29.	Compensation, district fixes	..	..	1
30.	Compensation, none to members	10	10	11
31.	Compensation, statute fixes	2	2	2
32.	Compensation act, workman's, must abide by.........	..	1	1
33.	Compulsory attendance laws, provide enforcement.....	13	14	15
34.	Consolidate schools, has power to...................	3	5	6
35.	Contracts, specified amounts must be written.........	6	6	5
36.	Contracts, make necessary and proper as per law.....	6	8	8

TABLE III (*Continued*)

No.	Brief Statement of the Laws	1901	1911	1921
37.	Convey property when it is sold	11	9	10
38.	County system obtains, local board, "listening post"	3	3	3
39.	Court, designated as for school disputes	2	1	1
40.	Course of study, must enforce	7	9	11
41.	Course of study, prescribes and enforces	13	16	16
42.	Curricula, extend to meet the needs	3	4	8
43.	Debts, must pay of boards superseded	3	5	7
44.	Debts, refund to secure better terms	2	3	5
45.	Dentists, appoint as needed	..	1	3
46.	Diplomas, grant to high school graduates	2	3	2
47.	Depositories, secure for school funds	1	4	5
48.	Dismiss for cause, teachers, superintendent, employees	15	22	20
49.	District, carry out instructions from	2	1	2
50.	Districts, establish and define boundaries of	1	1	2
51.	Divide city for election and other purposes	2	6	3
52.	Elections, arrange for holding	3	6	9
53.	Eminent domain, has right of	10	12	13
54.	Enumeration (census) cause to be taken annually	17	23	22
55.	Equipment, provide fixtures, fuel, libraries, etc.	20	23	23
56.	Establish new schools	6	6	5
57.	Estimates, make preliminary to all outlays	1	1	2
58.	Estimates, must submit to city council or others	..	2	3
59.	Escheated property goes to board for schools	1	1	1
60.	Evening schools, establish and maintain	6	10	14
61.	Examination-promotion system, provide for pupils	3	7	6
62.	Exclude pupils of non-age	4	2	3
63.	Expenditures, make limited without bids	2	2	3
64.	Expenses of board, board pays	1	1	1
65.	Extra-curricular activities, direct property to be used for.	..	1	3
66.	Fire laws, enforce and regulate hazards	1	1	5
67.	Flag, must provide for each building	9	12	13
68.	Fraternities, control or prohibit	1	4	8
69.	Gifts, (a) may accept; (b) may not accept	3	3	6
70.	Health and morals of pupils, must protect	4	8	9
71.	Health, have regular program for	2	3	9
72.	High school, establish and maintain	15	22	21
73.	High school building, rent only on vote	1	..	1
74.	Hire all employees other than teachers	14	17	18
75.	Hire all teachers	27	28	32
76.	Hours, fix for opening and closing school	4	4	4
77.	Incompatible office holders ineligible	2	5	4
78.	Institutes, teacher, provide or conduct	..	..	2
79.	Insure school property	10	8	9
80.	Journal of own proceedings, must keep	7	11	10
81.	Junior high school, establish and maintain	1	3	5
82.	Junior college, establish and maintain	..	..	1
83.	Kindergartens, establish and maintain	11	15	19
84.	Language, foreign, add to curricula	3	4	2
85.	Language, foreign, have school in	..	..	1
86.	Law, require all teachers to conform to	5	4	8
87.	Law, the equal pay, must abide by	..	1	1
88.	Law, general applies where not inconsistent	13	16	18
89.	Librarians, board appoints	5	10	7
90.	Libraries, establish and maintain	4	4	11
91.	Libraries, enforce rules and regulations of	5	5	6
92.	Libraries, exclude undesirable works	9	9	9

TABLE III (*Continued*)

No.	Brief Statement of the Laws	1901	1911	1921
93.	Litigation, conduct when directed by district	5	5	6
94.	Loans, make for operating expenses	1	2	1
95.	Lots, select and purchase at discretion	6	8	11
96.	Lots, sell at discretion	2	5	7
97.	Meetings, call public to determine policy	6	9	7
98.	Meetings, hold regular with notice	17	21	22
99.	Meetings, hold special with notice	14	15	16
100.	Members, contract with is void *ab initio*	13	15	15
101.	Military training, may provide for	2	2	4
102.	Minutes, must keep of meeting	5	5	6
103.	Money, must keep in designated depository	1	1	2
104.	Municipal university, establish and maintain	..	2	2
105.	Narcotics and poisons, require effects taught	6	6	7
106.	Non-existent, has no general law for cities	1	1	1
107.	Non-, mal- or misfeasance, wilful, carries penalty	4	5	5
108.	Oath, administer to teachers and employees	2	3	3
109.	Oath, required of members, stated or implied	21	23	22
110.	Oath not required, so stated or implied	1	1	1
111.	Obligations paid only on order of board	11	12	16
112.	Offices, board shall maintain	2	2	2
113.	Organize and elect its own officers	26	27	29
114.	Pension system, establish or administer	..	1	6
115.	Physicians, appoint as needed	..	6	8
116.	Physical education, provide for	2	6	9
117.	Primary pupils, authorize early dismissal	5	4	3
118.	Property, city council buys all	1	2	2
119.	Property, board manages all	22	24	27
120.	Property, board purchases on discretion	10	10	11
121.	Property, purchases when so voted	6	5	9
122.	Property, sells on discretion	12	14	15
123.	Property, sells when so voted	3	3	4
124.	Psychologist, clinical, appoint as needed	..	..	2
125.	Pupils, assign to state normal for practice	1	1	1
126.	Qualifications, judge of for new members	2	2	2
127.	Quorum, majority or larger number designated	11	12	15
128.	Ratifies teachers nominated by superintendent	3	3	4
129.	Real estate, power to "hold" for schools	6	7	5
130.	Recall, members subject to	2	2	4
131.	Recreational grounds, buy, establish, maintain	1	4	8
132.	Register of pupils, require teachers to keep	12	11	10
133.	Register of pupil applicants, board keeps	1	1	2
134.	Registry of bonds, board keeps	1	1	2
135.	Relatives, nepotism restricted or prohibited	4	6	8
136.	Rent property for school purposes	14	18	18
137.	Rent school property out	5	5	7
138.	Repair school property	17	23	22
139.	Report, make annual and publish same	11	12	12
140.	Report, make annual to county superintendent	10	10	13
141.	Report, make annual to state department	8	13	16
142.	Report, make annual to city officials	..	1	1
143.	Report, make as required by state board	3	3	4
144.	Report, make as required by superiors	7	10	11
145.	Rules and regulations, make for own government	20	20	19
146.	Rules and regulations, make for gov't of schools	26	27	25
147.	Rules and regulations, enforce those of state dept.	6	4	4
148.	Salaries, fix for employees, including teachers	17	23	21

TABLE III (*Continued*)

No.	Brief Statement of the Laws	1901	1911	1921
149.	Salary schedule, establish and abide by	1	1	2
150.	Schools, establish and maintain adequate	16	17	18
151.	Schools, establish and maintain parental	2	2	4
152.	Schools, establish and maintain vacational	1	1	5
153.	Seal, must keep and use seal	3	3	2
154.	Secretary non-member, hire and fix salary	13	11	13
155.	Secretary, member, hire and fix salary	3	4	4
156.	Secretary, member or non-, elect and fix salary	10	12	12
157.	Separate schools, provide for the races	5	7	7
158.	Sinking fund, invest according to law	3	4	6
159.	Sinking fund, must provide for	6	7	6
160.	Sites, locate or change location of	8	9	12
161.	Sue and be sued (body-corporate powers)	22	20	21
162.	Suits are in the name of the city	..	1	2
163.	Summer school, establish and maintain	2	2	3
164.	Superintendent, hire and fix salary	20	30	29
165.	Superintendent, reserve his decisions on supervision	2	3	3
166.	Supervision, board has but not control	1	1	1
167.	Supplies, purchase or provide	14	18	18
168.	Suspend and expel pupils for misconduct	16	18	18
169.	Tax, appoint collectors	1	2	2
170.	Tax, certify levy to public officials	11	10	11
171.	Tax, levy limited library taxes	2	2	3
172.	Tax, levy limited special taxes	5	5	6
173.	Tax, must levy for contingent fund	2	1	1
174.	Tax, submit proposed special levy to district vote	3	4	11
175.	Tax, unrestricted right to levy legal taxes	8	7	3
176.	Teacherages, erect, control and repair	..	1	3
177.	Teachers, certified, employ only	6	7	11
178.	Teachers, determine the number of	8	5	6
179.	Teachers, determine the qualifications of	4	4	4
180.	Teachers, examine, license, or have done	8	14	9
181.	Teachers, nominate to some higher authority	2	3	2
182.	Term, determine the length of	13	11	14
183.	Textbooks, provide all for indigent poor	9	9	11
184.	Textbooks, change according to law	7	8	8
185.	Textbooks, provide free by district vote	5	4	6
186.	Textbooks, provide all free, law so states	9	12	13
187.	Textbooks, provide free at option	3	5	7
188.	Textbooks, require as condition to admission	4	1	2
189.	Textbooks, select and prescribe	14	16	13
190.	Textbooks, sell to pupils desiring to purchase	5	4	6
191.	Toilets, provide suitable separate	6	7	7
192.	Transfer pupils when advisable	8	7	9
193.	Transportation, provide when advisable	8	9	14
194.	Treasurer, city treasurer acts ex-officio	6	8	10
195.	Treasurer, county treasurer acts ex-officio	3	4	4
196.	Treasurer, board elects and fills vacancies	6	6	5
197.	Unit, board must act as and not as individuals	1	1	2
198.	Vacancies, permanently filled by board	4	3	3
199.	Vacancies, temporarily filled by the board	18	17	18
200.	Vaccination, provide and require	6	4	4
201.	Visit, board must as specified	16	20	19
202.	Vocational schools, establish and maintain	5	9	12
203.	Water supply, provide for	2	2	2
204.	Warrants of teachers, must not discount	2	3	4

number of states, are relatively small. Consequently any small increase or decrease in these totals between 1901 and 1911, or 1911 and 1921, is indicative of a considerable trend in the development of school legislation in the direction so indicated.

The original data from which Table III was derived consist of the "Brief Statement of the Laws," against which has been entered the index number of each state, in whose school codes the given law was found for the years 1901, 1911 and 1921. In reading Table III it must be remembered that only the school codes were analyzed. The writer is not unmindful of the fact that laws definitely affecting education are often found in other codes. To illustrate, laws affecting school attendance might be found in, or construed from, the penal codes of the state.

SUMMARY

The conditions disclosed by Table III and by the research described in this chapter are summarized as follows:

1. There seems to be no discoverable system common among the states by which the numerous provisions of the statutory school laws have come into existence. Probably it was a trial and error method that first produced them. Later, one state would copy another, and probably following that state from which its most influential pioneers had migrated.

2. There is a tendency to enact the school law into more detailed form in the period from 1901 to 1911 and on to 1921.

3. There is already a very wide range of variation in school laws which set forth the powers and duties of city school boards and there have been some attempts to select for intrinsic worth from this great variety. The code of California is an example of this tendency.

4. There are, however, too many archaic and useless provisions allowed to remain as a part of the *corpus juris* of schools. This practice of retaining obsolete law obscures the more modern provisions and thereby lessens, if not abrogates, their effect.

5. There is an increasing tendency to grant to boards of education as agents of the state, the sole power to levy school taxes and to expend the income thereof, and to secure the right to levy exceptionally high taxes by submitting the question to vote of the people.

6. There appears to be a slight tendency for the legislatures to designate boards of education as policy formulating agents, and to require that the executive work be done by experts.

7. There is rather a strong tendency to grant boards of education the power to extend the scope of the schools, to establish all sorts of special schools, recreational grounds, etc.; and to allow them to purchase textbooks and other school supplies in ever increasing quantities.

8. In states which have radically revised their law for city districts recently, there is a strong tendency to enact into the statutes the suggestions as to powers and duties of boards which are made in the several city school surveys.

9. Growth in legal enactment lags behind actual practice in educational affairs. This is because the legal provision must have some sort of prototype, either as a vision, or as an actual performance. Likewise, the fact that "Men are prone to suffer while the evils are sufferable rather than to disturb the even tenor of their ways," is an additional cause of this lethargy.

10. As a consequence of this apathy in legal reform, the slight changes that do occur indicate a much stronger trend than would otherwise appear to be the case.

11. It is evident that the legislative power of the courts, that is, their power to modify and alleviate the evils of legislation by construction thereof, and by the adjudication of specific cases which then become precedents, is to a very great extent relied upon by the friends of education, to safeguard its interests.

CHAPTER VII

FUNDAMENTAL LEGAL PRINCIPLES PERTAINING TO CITY SCHOOL BOARDS AND ESTABLISHED THROUGH RESEARCH AND EXPERT OPINION

PURPOSES OF THIS CHAPTER

It is purposed in this chapter to compile and organize the fundamental legal provisions which pertain to city school boards. Obviously, these cannot consist of untried theories. They must be chosen from the past and present practices in the various sections of the nation. To accomplish this end, it is necessary:

1. To ascertain a source from which to obtain the material.
2. To secure some criteria by which to evaluate the intrinsic worth of the material selected.
3. To use criteria that are already generally accepted as logical units of measurement for the given material; or else justify them so that they will be thus accepted.

THE CITY SCHOOL SURVEYS AS SOURCES AND THE EVALUATION OF THEIR SUGGESTIONS AS POTENTIAL PRACTICE

Investigation discloses that the published surveys * of the various city school systems will serve as such a source; and any legal principle, or provision, advocated or recommended in them is *prima facie* evidence of a general tendency to accept it as fundamentally sound. In support of this position, it is to be noted that nowhere else is there such a volume of expert criticism and constructive suggestion based on actual conditions as is to be found in these surveys. In them exhaustive research has been made and the results interpreted into practicable suggestions.

With the principles underlying the making of school law, as

* Surveys will be referred to by cities. A complete bibliography with full titles is given in Appendix III, under references for Chapter VII.

set forth in Chapter IV, more or less developed, with the history of city boards and their practices in mind, and guided by the knowledge that, as a legal entity, the board is a *quasi* corporation, it was possible for the surveyor to do his work in a city after the manner of an experiment in an actual life situation. In the making of a survey, worthy of the name, are all of the vital and necessary elements for determining the best possible legal provisions for the control and government of a school system under a city board of education. Most important among these are:

1. There is available the history of the efficiency of any given law.
2. The actual function of any given law may be observed.
3. The variability of laws in the various cities of the same size make comparative studies possible.
4. A list of court decisions is available, which have operated somewhat after the fashion of the law of the survival of the fittest.
5. Use is made of modern scientific measuring instruments for determining results.
6. Lists of schemes whereby the real intent of the law has, in the past, been subverted.
7. The personnel of the directors and assistant directors of the surveys has been composed of the most expert investigators of school problems. They have worked in a scientific way to diagnose the present condition of the particular school system, and prescribed, among other things, the remedial legislation required to raise the system to an optimum of efficiency. Among other things they have quite generally:

a. Recognized professional standing.
b. Long periods of successful school experience.
c. A knowledge of the modern psychology of learning.
d. An acquaintance with the other tools of modern educational practices.
e. A knowledge of the best technique for making such studies.

From this exposition, it would seem justifiable to select, as good potential legal practice, the recommendations found in the several surveys. The order of statement is based on chronological occurrence of the particular provision as it most likely would appear in the law creating and defining the powers and duties of city boards of education. Such order is in no way indicative of the relative values of the several recommendations.

Reiteration of any given recommendation serves, in a measure, as an index of its importance. This is true even though the same thought is quoted from the same source. Obviously the more frequently any principle is advocated in published form, the greater will be the number of readers into whose hands it will come, and the greater the possibility that the proposal will be challenged.

WHAT THE SURVEYS ADVOCATE

Constitutional Provisions

1. The people of a state, through the medium of their state constitutions, should charge their respective legislatures with the imperative obligation of providing for a complete and adequate system of free schools, publicly supported and controlled, extending in scope from and including the kindergarten through the university. This system should be adequate and free to all the children of the state regardless of race, nationality or sex. Each of the forty-eight states has a more or less effectual clause of this character in its constitution.[1]

The constitution of the State of New York requires that the legislature provide for "a system of free common schools wherein all the children of the state may be educated." By this provision of the constitution and by the decisions of the courts education is recognized as a function of the state. *Watertown, N. Y.*, p. 1.

2. The constitution should declare education to be a state, not a local, function. The members of the board of education are then, without question, as the courts have declared them to be, state and not municipal officers. As such they should be independent fiscally and in all other ways of municipal control.

Public education is a function of the state government, and a city board of school control is the delegated power of the state to administer state laws relative to public education. As such the city board of school control should administer in full its own financial affairs. *Winston-Salem, N. C.*, p. 4.

The charter should be changed so that the board of education may levy taxes for the support of the schools. *Memphis, Tenn.*, p. 49.

The power of the board of education to carry out its plans for the extension and improvement of the schools depends upon the action of an independent body, which can have no such intimate knowledge of the school's needs as has the board of education. *Wilmington, Del.*, p. 26.

The fact that public education is a function of the state and that the schools are the chief instruments provided for the development of social progress justifies the separation of the school administration from the general municipal administration. One may very properly propose that the success of all local, state, and national government is dependent upon the work done in the schools. It is appropriate that the administration of these schools be kept distinct from those political considerations which so often control in municipal affairs. *Watertown, N. Y.*, p. 1.

In the one group of cities the board of education acts as a separate corporation, has the power to raise school revenues within a limit commonly fixed by state law, and has complete control of the spending of the funds thus made available. . . .

The dual control of schools thus established has caused dissatisfaction upon the part of the School Committee, the Council, and interested citizens. *Providence, R. I.*, p. 7.

In the study of the situation in Providence, we have had the benefit of an investigation which considered the situation in 377 American cities. In a report of an investigation with respect to the financing of education in American municipalities, Dr. J. R. McGaughy shows that the boards of education which are responsible for raising revenues and for spending the funds so secured are maintaining their schools at a slightly lower average cost per pupil in average daily attendance than are the cities in which the school budget is controlled by the board of estimate or other municipal authority. It was discovered as well that 70 per cent of these boards of education, which had the right to determine the tax levy for schools, had as a matter of fact fixed a tax rate well within the limit established by law. *Providence, R. I.*, p. 9.

No educational policy of significance can be determined out of relation to the issue of financing the program. . . .

A school committee cannot pass upon important questions of policy except as they are able to determine within a limit established by law the amount of money to be spent. *Providence, R. I.*, p. 10.

If satisfactory results are to be secured, the highest degree of coöperation must exist between the professional staff of the School Committee and those responsible for the operation and maintenance of the school buildings. It seems obvious, therefore, that the final responsibility of these employees should rest with the School Committee. *Providence, R. I.*, p. 12.

Few boards of education can be charged with over-emphasizing education and with expending an unjustifiably large amount of money on their public school organizations. *Marion, Ill.*, p. 53.

Because of the methods of securing funds for the support of education, American cities are commonly grouped into two classes, those which are fiscally independent and those which are fiscally dependent. The fiscally independent school systems are those which levy their own tax, determine their own budget subdivisions and expend their funds, being directly responsible to the people of the community. The fiscally dependent school systems are those which, like that of Stamford, must submit their budget to another local municipal authority for revision. These cities in which the school systems are directly dependent financially upon a second budget approximate 26 per cent of all American municipalities.

In a study made during the current school year, it was discovered that fiscally independent school systems do not expend any greater amounts per pupil in average daily attendance than do dependent cities. There is a distinct tendency for tax rates for school purposes to be higher in independent cities, but this is because of the fact that dependent cities are much more inclined to incur bonded indebtedness both for school and municipal purposes. That is to say, independent cities tend very definitely "to pay as they go."

Independent cities provide much more adequate school plants for the pupils. Not only is there a larger percentage of the school children adequately housed in school buildings owned by the city, but there is also much more adequate provision for playground space. Independent cities have likewise been much more successful in holding their children in school beyond the ages of compulsory attendance. Another factor of importance in favor of independence of Boards of Education is the fact that during the period of rapid increase in the cost of living from 1913 to 1920, such boards were able to increase the salary of teachers more nearly to conformity with the advance in the cost of living. These are some of the measures on which comparable data could be secured. It is the general opinion of those who have been students of school administration over a long period of time that schools are more successful when operated by fiscally independent school boards.

The reports submitted, covering all phases of school development in Stamford, lead to the conclusion that the system of financial control under which the school committee has been operating has not been securing the best educational results in the local school system. *Stamford, Conn.*, p. 11.

Instead of leaving the maintenance of schools to community option, their maintenance has been required; instead of leaving the levying of taxes to the whims of town or city councils, the boards of school trustees have been given independent power to levy a school tax; . . .

The courts, too, have uniformly decided the school districts are separate and distinct corporations from municipal corporations with which they may be contiguous or may form a part. Municipal corporations exist for the purposes of local governments, and are largely local affairs; school corporations exist for the purpose of carrying out a state purpose, are largely independent of local control, and are under the supervision of a special department of the state government. *Butte, Mont.*, p. 110.

Even in districts of the first class the powers of the school board come from the state and not from the city; its authority to act comes from a state school law; and its limitations are imposed by the state. . . . These state regulations have been prescribed largely in an effort to protect the schools from the attacks or the neglect of short-sighted communities. . . . *Butte, Mont.*, p. 111.

The city Board of Education is in reality a state organization located in a municipality. It is not a city department provided for in the city charges in the same way as are the police, fire and welfare departments. *Butte, Mont.*, pp. 18-19.

Functions of the Legislature: Scope of Authority and Responsibility. The constitutional obligation to provide a system of public schools should be mandatory. The legislature, as the state's agent for creating schools, should be obliged to enact the necessary legislation for carrying out the following necessary implications of the people's will in regard to education:

Districts. They should by general law provide for the creation and modification of city school districts in the following particulars:

1. The laying out of a district, which, whenever desirable, would not be coterminous with the city but would extend beyond the city limits;
2. The organization thereof;
3. Subsequent necessary changes thereof;
4. Provision for holding elections:
    a. To elect a board of education;
    b. To determine policies by popular vote.

Even when the boundaries of a school district are one and the same as those of a municipal corporation, the intent of the law, and the decisions of the courts in a number of states, are that the school district is a separate and distinct corporation from the municipality, and created for a different purpose. The municipality exists largely for local ends; the school district exists largely for the carrying out of a state purpose. *Portland, Ore.*, pp. 5-6.

The district is numbered and takes its legal name from the county and state organization; its powers all come from the state; it could be changed in form or purpose at any time by the state; and it exists primarily for the carrying out of a purpose which our American states long ago decided to be in the interests of the state. *Portland, Ore.*, p. 7.

The law should in addition provide for a good modern educational organization for such a city, and should specify the main powers of the Board, the Superintendent of Schools, the Superintendent of Properties and the Clerk or Secretary. Certain powers and duties should be guaranteed to each, and they should be safeguarded in the exercise of them by law. The right of the district to make its own courses of study, to adopt its own textbooks, to set its own requirements for entering the teaching service, to contract with its own teachers, and to establish such schools and such types of educational activity as seem needed, should be included in the law as a matter of course. The right to determine the rate or the amount of school taxes to be levied, up to certain maxima, for buildings, equipment and annual maintenance, ought to be given to the Board of School Directors alone, and with the further right to submit the question to a vote of the people if, in their judgment, still larger sums are needed to meet emergencies or special educational needs. *Portland, Ore.*, p. 8.

What the state should be primarily interested in is that certain minimum standards should be met, and not in limiting new efforts of communities. *Portland, Ore.*, p. 9.

The board owes its existence to a state law and its powers and duties are closely defined and limited by state legislation. The city Board of Education is in reality a state organization located in a municipality. It is not a city department provided for in the city charter in the same way as are the police, fire and welfare departments. The city of Cleveland is practically free to have such fire and police departments as it pleases. It could, if it wished, readily change the organization of either or both. It paves its streets as it thinks wise and if the people thought best they might decide to have no parks at all or twice as many as at prseent.

In dealing with public education the city enjoys no such liberty of action. The state of Ohio, like most other American commonwealths, has considered education a matter of general importance and far-reaching consequence and has not left it wholly to the management of individual municipalities. It has not only decreed that the maintenance of public schools shall be universally obligatory, but it has enacted detailed legislation prescribing the organization of the Board of Education, the methods by which it shall raise funds, the ways in which it shall do business, the number and even the salaries of the employees it may engage, the kinds of education it may maintain, the time the schools shall remain open, the way in which books shall be selected, and so on through a long list of items as to the manner in which public education shall be organized and maintained.

If the state legislature so wishes, it may modify the powers and duties of the Board of Education. It could change the organization of the board or even do away with it entirely and erect some other agency in its stead. If the people of the city think the board should have new or different powers, they cannot make the change through the city council but must instead apply to the state legislature. When the board finds that its funds are not sufficient, as is at present the case, it can get them increased only by securing a change in the state laws. *Cleveland, Ohio*, pp. 19-20.

The object of the state in providing for a Board of Education is not to appoint the members to manage the schools, but rather to create a small body of citizens that shall represent the whole community, and that shall in turn employ competent executive officers to organize and manage the school system. The fundamental purpose of the state law is that the educational policies shall be determined by the board and that they shall be put into execution by the professional administrative officers employed by the board. *Cleveland, Ohio,* p. 21.

Prescribe and Fix the Legal Status of City School Boards. The Legislature should by general law prescribe and fix the status of the City Board of Education.

1. The Board of Education should be elected from the city at large, on a non-partisan ballot, and at an independent or special school election.

However well it may have worked in Salt Lake City, the ward system is nevertheless undesirable and has been abandoned by many cities. The almost universal experience has been that board members have averaged higher from the city at large than when elected along ward lines, and petty local politics and local feelings influence the board less in its actions. The school system of a city is a unit and board members should represent this larger unit and not some portion of it. *Salt Lake City, Utah,* p. 34-5.

The Watertown Board of Education should be elected directly by the people of Watertown and should be completely independent of the local municipal government both in determining the amount of the local school tax and in expending all school revenue. *Watertown, N. Y.,* p. 7.

The Board of Education which should be responsible directly to the electorate of the school district is responsible to the mayor, and the city council has power to review the budget. *Watertown, N. Y.,* p. 21.

A Board of Education should be elected at large on a non-partisan ticket by the citizens of Watertown. *Watertown, N. Y.,* p. 26.

The practice in American cities arrived at out of the experience of the past fifty years and more favors the election of a small school committee of from five to nine members from the city at large. Many cities that have elected their school committee by wards have changed their method during the past two decades. This change has occurred because they have believed that it was more possible to secure the services of competent citizens when the selection is made without reference to the residence of these persons within the divisions of the political subdivisions of the city.

The election of school committee members from wards or districts implies that the members elected from the several sections of the city are to be particularly concerned with the educational interests of that part of the city from which they are elected. This idea involves two fallacies: The one that a school board member should favor his locality rather than consider the needs of the whole city, and the other that school committee members are to be responsible for recommending the details of the educational program to be carried out, or for the execution of that program. It seems unfortunate to suggest that any member of a school committee would favor the children of his locality rather than consider the needs of the whole city. No efficient administration of schools can be developed if school committee members believe it is their responsibility to initiate school policy, or to carry into execution the program adopted by the whole committee. Both of these functions belong to the professional staff employed by the school committee. *Providence, R. I.*, pp. 15-16.

Students of public administration have long opposed the placing of members on school boards by virtue of the holding of an office to which they have been elected which does not relate to the work of the school committee. An examination of the minutes of the Providence School Committee shows that the ex-officio members do not take any considerable part in the activities of the School Committee. This is as one would expect it to be. Neither the Mayor nor the President of the Common Council in a city the size of Providence, with the other responsibilities which they have, can be expected to meet with the School Committee or to spend any considerable time in the consideration of the problems which come before this body. It will be observed in the draft of the law given above that it is proposed to reduce the committee to seven members and that the ex-officio members are omitted. *Providence, R. I.*, p. 16.

Under the present law board members are chosen at popular elections held at the same time as the elections for city officers. It is clear that this is not the wisest method of selecting a board of education. In the excitement of the general election the welfare of the schools becomes temporarily a matter of minor consideration and school interests are obscured by political interests.

A much better way is to hold the school elections at a separate time from the other elections. This change has been put into effect in a number of cities and has been found a great improvement over the old way. If the school elections are held quietly each spring in public school houses and with a simplified form of ballot, it is found that the expense is slight in comparison with the beneficial results that are brought about. *Cleveland, Ohio*, p. 122-3.

Another device for securing the same results is to have the board members appointed by the mayor or elected by the city commissioners instead of having them elected by the people. Under a commission form of government, election by the commissioners gives exceedingly satisfactory results, but under the ordinary form of city government, popular election on a special election day is probably the best plan. *Cleveland, Ohio*, p. 123.

School elections should not be held simultaneously with municipal elections, and the city should seek a change in the law so as to provide for school elections on some other date or providing a substitute for popular election. *Cleveland, Ohio*, p. 135.

2. All citizens, legal residents of the city, and over 21 years of age should be electors for all school elections; and eligible for election to membership on the board of education.

3. The board of education should consist of five (or seven) members, chosen for a term of not less than five years; and the

order of the election should be so arranged that only one full term member may be elected at each annual election.

The members of the school committee should be public-spirited men and women of wide experience and of sound common sense. *Providence, R. I.*, p. 25.

The fact that the board of education is made up of successful business men shows that prominent citizens have enough interest to give a part of their time to directing the activities of the schools. *Marion, Ill.*, p. 9.

The School Committee of thirty-three members elected by the citizens of Providence, or a smaller committee selected in like manner may be expected to represent the people of the city as well as any other municipal body. Within the limits determined by the constitution, which denies to members of boards elected by all of the voters the right to appropriate money, the members of the School Committee, by virtue of the mandate given them by the electorate, should be made responsible for the financing and administration of all school activities. *Providence, R. I.*, p. 3.

There are nine members of the Board of School Commissioners who serve without pay and whose term of office is six years. The length of term, the small number of board members and the fact that there is no financial remuneration for service on the Board of Education are elements conforming to the best educational practice. As far as the Survey Commission is able to ascertain, the Baltimore Board of School Commissioners is unique in that their President is appointed by the mayor of the city. *Baltimore, Md.*, Vol. II, p. 19.

As a matter of fact, even a large board of 12 or 15 members can personally represent but a few of the many social and vocational classes in the community. The way to take care of the many points of view is not to fill up the board with a large number of men; it is rather to choose carefully a very few men of sound judgment who know the community and the needs of the community, and whose business or other affiliations are not such as to limit their independence or judgment. These men can then at open meetings hear the claims of every interested class. *South Bend, Ind.*, p. 208.

Frequent elections under the old system (two-year term) led to many short terms, and consequently to a lack of the necessary continuity of service to produce high efficiency. The new method of election for four years is sure to work a helpful reform along this line. *Leavenworth, Kan.*, p. 28.

It goes without saying that, even with the best of intentions, with the best of intelligence, and the best of other qualifications, a school board is greatly handicapped if a majority of its members have had less than a year's experience and familiarity with the school affairs of the system. *El Paso, Texas*, p. 13.

A board of five, one that could meet in a smaller room and around a single table, and with more board and less committee action would handle the educational business more quickly and more efficiently than a board of 10 members, and with fewer conflicts with its executive officers and fewer reversals of action. A large board almost always leads to unnecessary discussion and often has to reverse itself. *Salt Lake City, Utah,* p. 35.

4. Vacancies occurring should be filled by the remaining members of the board, immediately, and until the next annual election, at which time the said vacancy should be filled by regular election for the unexpired term.

In case a vacancy shall occur in a Board of Education, the Board shall appoint to fill the vacancy, the person so appointed to serve until the next annual school election, at which time a member shall be elected to fill out the unexpired term of the member. *Portland, Ore.,* p. 314.

5. All unnecessary formality in connection with placing a name on the nonpartisan ballot should be dispensed with. A petition signed by a very few electors should be sufficient. This will tend to eliminate the savor of politics and induce persons of high caliber to stand for election, who might otherwise refuse to become involved in what they consider petty politics.

Citizens of the highest type are often willing to serve on boards of education when they would not be willing to enter the field of municipal politics. If, as is commonly the practice, the term on the board of education is five years or more, the individual member comes into the board, a majority of whom have served for a number of years, and participates in the development of a policy which continues without regard to change in the political control of the city. *Watertown, N. Y.,* pp. 1-2.

We need on Boards of Education men and women of good judgment, of wide experience, and of sound common sense. They can and should check the executive officer who may become too enthusiastic or who would carry too heavy a load of experimentation in any given period. It is just as certain that they should, when convinced of the wisdom of the policies proposed by the Superintendent of Schools, support him not only in board meetings, but before the community at large. A policy once adopted they should consider their policy as well as that of the Superintendent of Schools. *Watertown, N. Y.,* p. 19.

In general such efficient board members are men who are successful in handling large and difficult undertakings. They are often merchants, manufacturers, bankers, contractors, and professional men of large practice. *Cleveland, Ohio,* p. 123.

6. In the states where the fiscal year begins July 1, the school election for Board members should be held in the late spring, preferably in May, so that the newly elected member, or members,

may have time to qualify and take office at the beginning of the fiscal year.

Meetings of the City School Board. The general school law should specify regular monthly meetings for the board, leaving it optional for them to call special meetings when necessary; but, the general practice of holding special meetings should not be encouraged.

1. The first meeting in July should be termed the annual meeting, at which time, in addition to the regular business thereof, the new members should take the oath of office, and begin their duties as members.

Organization of the City Board. The following organization, or some organization not inconsistent with the following, should be prescribed by the legislature, for the city board of education.

At the annual meeting, the board should elect a president for the ensuing year, a vice president, a treasurer; and should designate the head clerk of the superintendent's office as the secretary of the board. This will necessitate having a highly qualified person, capable of taking large responsibilities, in that office. The clerk is originally selected by the superintendent, and the appointment confirmed by the board. Ability and permanency being highly desirable in this office, appointment for longer periods than one year will be good practice.

In general, it may be said that many features of the organization under the board of education and the superintendent of schools are excellent. The principal suggestion is that the committee organization under the board of education might be largely eliminated under a reorganization placing the larger responsibility on the chief executive representative of the board, the superintendent of schools. This involves at the same time the enlarging of the functions of the clerk of the board, who, under the general direction of the superintendent of schools, should be given larger responsibility in connection with business matters. *Lockport, N. Y.*, pp. 23-24.

Committees of Boards of Education. The general law should specifically prohibit standing committees, but permit the appointment of special committees for specific purposes, the accomplishment of which should automatically discharge them.

Few matters of educational policy are considered by the board and most of these have their origin in outside sources. . . . The first of these is to be found in the legal provisions as to board procedure. The second consists of the way in which the board conducts its business through committees.

There does not seem to be any good reason for this type of organization. In most boards consisting of a large number of members there are numerous committees which carry on much of the real deliberation about the different subjects considered. Experience has amply demonstrated that the big board with the numerous committees represents an ineffective and inefficient form of organization . . . it has been found that the big city must have a small Board of Education because its business is big and requires informed, united, and energetic action on the part of those who conduct it. This is impossible where the big board is split up into a large number of little committees handling many detailed matters and tending to become independent of each other.

Because of these reasons the small board has replaced the large one precisely for the purpose of making it possible for the board to act as a committee of the whole.

The board itself has largely nullified the hoped for advantage of the new organization by dividing itself into numerous committees and building up the tradition that almost every new matter to be considered shall first be passed upon by a committee consisting of three members out of the seven and immediately thereafter passed upon by all seven members. . . . The procedure of referring each question to a committee is largely one of form and is seriously time-consuming.

Indeed, many competent students of the subject have come to the conclusion that the board does not need permanent committees for the exercise of its legislative functions. Where there are only seven members, most business can be readily transacted by the board as a whole and such committees as are appointed are purely temporary. Some large cities have recently adopted this plan. *Cleveland, Ohio,* pp. 53-64.

As a conclusion of this (committee) consideration the statement is made that the present procedure through committees is one of the factors mainly responsible for loading up the board with a mass of routine and detailed work. There is ample evidence that the board's business would be far more simply and readily conducted if most of it were transacted directly by the board as a whole without being referred to the committees. *Cleveland, Ohio,* pp. 130-1.

The board should simplify and largely abandon its present method of conducting business through committees. *Cleveland, Ohio,* p. 135.

The recommendation made by the survey committee involves the elimination of all such committees, the board itself meeting as a committee of the whole to discuss matters that need informal discussion before the formulation of a policy. In this way every member of the board would be thoroughly familiar with every policy before it is finally approved. From time to time as need arises special committees may be appointed which will perform specific tasks assigned them by the board and then cease to exist when that specific duty has been performed. If purely routine and executive matters are delegated to the professional executives employed by the board, then the board will have time to discuss in detail the policies to be formulated, and give attention to the planning of a comprehensive program for the future as well as for the present. *Watertown, N. Y.*, p. 14.

It has been proposed by those familiar with the work of the present School Committee that the Executive Committee is in effect a small school committee. The other standing committees are made up of five members each. There are eighteen of these committees, designated as follows: Accounts, annual report, apportionment, by-laws, evening schools, free public lectures, grammar and primary schools, high schools, hygiene, industrial education and drawing, military training, music, penmanship, private schools, relations to the City Council, schoolhouses, special schools, summer schools.

In addition to these standing committees there are ten ward committees, each of which is composed of three members elected from the ward. In addition to these the School Committee from time to time creates special committees. . . .

When the final report comes from the standing committee of last reference the School Committee as a whole almost invariably adopts the report. . . . This misunderstanding of the function of the School Committee is further evidenced by the fact that the superintendent of schools seldom meets with many of the standing committees. *Providence, R. I.*, p. 17.

Practice concerning the number of standing committees included in the organization of city Boards of Education varies greatly. . . . If the school system of Baltimore is organized as is described elsewhere in this chapter, it will become unnecessary for the Board to continue these six standing committees. It is the opinion of the Survey Commission that the Board of School Commissioners may eliminate all of its standing committees and find that its service to the city of Baltimore has not been impaired. . . . As a rule, committees appointed to act as the need arises and discharged when their services are performed will tend toward a more expeditious advancement of the work of the Board of Education. *Baltimore, Md.*, Vol. II, p. 20.

Two committees—drifted apart into virtually two boards. *Grand Rapids, Mich.*, p. 479.

Argument against the five committees of the board but no survey of this phase was made. *Hackensack, N. J.*, p. 10.

There is no particular objection to the size of Boise's board, nor to its tenure and methods of election. There is, however, objection to the standing committee method of carrying on its work. For nearly a decade no single problem has received more serious consideration by our leading thinkers and writers on educational administration than has the question of how school boards shall conduct their business. The outcome of this study is a general agreement to the effect that standing committees are in no way helpful, and they are not infrequently a means of mismanagement and interference with the technical and professional functions of expert officers. As the plan works in Boise little concrete evidence was available to show any evil effects upon the schools direct. The committees are definitely subordinate to the board, having no general power to act on any question. Yet all the work done by committees might in the judgment of the writer, be better done in other ways. For a committee of three busy men to toil through the process of auditing the long list of large and small expenditures which accumulate each month seems extremely wasteful of time. Again, the selection, tenure, and salaries of teachers, the selection of text-books, questions of instruction and discipline, all are problems whose proper solution not only requires time but also a high degree of professional skill, such as lay board members usually do not possess.

Special committees may and frequently should be used by the board for examining situations, gathering facts, assisting in large business transactions, etc., but never should questions of any importance be either actually, or even practically decided by any less than the full membership of the board whom the people have chosen to manage the schools.

Without mentioning all the evils that have been found associated with committee methods, it is enough here to say that all are a possibility in Boise as soon as even moderately weak executive officers are placed in charge of the schools.

Boise's committees should be done away with, however, not only to prevent waste and friction but because there are better and safer methods of handling the business. *Boise, Idaho,* pp. 28-30.

The committee method of handling the business of the trustees is out of keeping with modern administrative theory and practice. That the rules of the board be so revised as to eliminate all standing committees, with a consequent enlargement of the executive power of the superintendent. . . . *Boise, Idaho,* p. 39.

The board should do away with its standing committees and operate as a board only. *Boise, Idaho,* p. 283.

Boise's administrative organization has been described and five important points of weakness pointed out, as follows:

1. The committee method of handling the business of the trustees is out of keeping with modern administrative theory and practice;

2. The placement of almost the entire supervision of instruction in the hands of the superintendent with one assistant, together with making all principals "head teachers" and leaving the superintendent too little time for important executive work, inevitably results in poor supervision and inadequate administration;

3. Lack of proper limitation of the duties of the building inspector, with a consequent wrong relationship between principals and janitors, creates serious trouble;

4. A wrong type of machinery for handling the problems of attendance tends to stimulate rather than to discourage delinquency;

5. Inadequate health supervision cannot but result from the present arrangement.

To correct these weak points in the system it is recommended:

1. That the rules of the board be so revised as to eliminate all standing committees, with a consequent enlargement of the executive powers of the

superintendent, the introduction of a budget system of finance and a definitely outlined policy touching the main problems that have constantly to be met by the superintendent;

2. That the idea of teaching principals be done away with, that the superintendent be freed from any save general supervision of all the schools, and that more special supervision be introduced;

3. That the title of building inspector be changed to that of superintendent of buildings and grounds, that he shall work under the direction of the superintendent rather than under the board or one of the board's committees, and that he shall have general supervision of all janitor service;

4. That attendance problems shall no longer be referred to the probation officer of the juvenile court, but that the school shall devise its own machinery for meeting that problem by adding an assistant, a "visiting teacher" to the office of the medical supervisor;

5. That the present nurse be made supervisor of health and attendance and be given an assistant.

With these changes it is believed that Boise would have a thoroughly modern administrative and supervisory machinery. The change would likely cost somewhat more, but it would undoubtedly result in a large increase in efficiency throughout the system. *Boise, Idaho,* pp. 39-40.

There are eight standing committees of the board of education: finance, teachers, buildings, grounds and janitors, supplies, course of study and manual training, libraries, rules, regulations and printing, and high school.

In the administration of the school organization many of the duties nominally assigned to one committee or another have been in large part delegated to their executive representatives—the superintendent of schools and the clerk of the board. The board in practice therefore recognizes the modern tendency in educational administration which has in large part eliminated the detail work of committee assignments through the placing of larger responsibilities on the executive officers of the board.

As the board functions in large part as a whole rather than through committees, serious consideration might well be given to the wisdom of doing away entirely with all committees. Notwithstanding the number of committees provided for in the by-laws, the board of education of Niagara Falls is not bound by committee procedure as is true in many cities. *Niagara Falls, N. Y.,* pp. 25-26.

The meetings of the board are congested with matters of administrative detail, many of which should be handled directly by the administrative office. . . .

The board is overorganized into committees which are expected to attend to matters belonging without question to the experts employed by the board. This is particularly true of the sub-committees of the committee on buildings and grounds, who authorize all incidental alterations and repairs. *Utica, N. Y.,* pp. 40-41.

There are six standing committees of the board of education: buildings and grounds; purchasing; teachers, school organization and government;

finance and accounts; rules, regulations, school census and elections; school health service, physical training and school athletics. The reports of committees frequently appear in the minutes of the board. While these committees have rendered an excellent service, many of their duties, however, are of an administrative character and should be delegated directly by the board to their executive representatives. *Lockport, N. Y.*, pp. 23-24.

The local committee organization of the School Committee may be abandoned without injury to the administration of school affairs. The number of standing committees should be reduced and preferably only two committees, if any, retained. The standing committees which render the most effective service and which are of the greatest assistance are the Committee on Finance and the Committee on Physical Plant. When Committee action is needed, it is recommended that committees be appointed as the need arises and discharged when their services are performed. *Stamford, Conn.*, p. 14.

With a small board there is little need for standing committees. *Janesville, Wis.*, p. 101.

It would be well if the law stated that the board must act finally in all cases as a unit.[2] Not to so act is illegal, but, since board members as a usual thing will be uninformed on this matter, it will prevent mistakes, if the statement is made in the school codes. General cognizance of this fact will also tend to show the futility of standing committees.

The committee on buildings and grounds acts chiefly as individuals, ordering repairs, painting, etc., without consultation and without previous action of the board. The committee meets, confirms the acts of the individual members, and then requests confirmation by the board. *Wheeling, W. Va.*, p. 10.

The Superintendent of Schools. The law should designate the city superintendent of schools as the chief executive of the board. He is not to be the president of the board, but the official who is the final executor of all school policies and other business.

The Superintendent of Schools is the professional leader of the entire school system. As such it is his function to act as general supervisory head coördinating the work of the various units to the end that there may be unity of aim and continuity of effort. But no one man can cover the entire field in the detail that is necessary to formulate educational aims, outline curricula to realize these aims, improve methods of teaching, supervise teachers for the purpose of improving them as professional workers, and measure the results of instruction. With almost two hundred teachers and more than a dozen buildings it is imperative that the Superintendent be supported by professionally trained assistants. . . . *Watertown, N. Y.*, p. 24.

The Board of Education should require the Superintendent of schools, as its chief officer, to assume responsibility for budgeting supplies, for determining the kind and quality of supplies and equipment needed and the purchase and proper distribution of the same. In the office of the assistant to the superintendent should be centralized all the details of budgeting, purchasing, distributing and accounting of supplies. The machinery for purchasing and distributing of supplies should be simple and efficient, of standard procedure, avoiding unnecessary delay and duplication of clerical work, showing each step of the transaction from source to culmination and guarding against waste or misuse of supplies.

There should be a permanent and continuing system of accounting which will show readily at any time the quantity of supplies on hand, the quantity distributed and where used. There should be a complete record of every transaction so that at any time one may have accurate knowledge of any situation as to appropriations, expenditures and bills outstanding. The record should be continuous and cumulative.

General supplies should be purchased on competitive bids but the Superintendent should have authority within limits to make special and emergency purchases without bids. Such special and emergency supplies should, however, be reduced to the minimum.

The main supplies in sufficient quantity to meet the needs of the entire year should be found in the various buildings, ready for use at the opening of schools in the fall. Accurate records of consumption of supplies per grade should be kept for each building, so as to enable those responsible for the preparation of the annual budget to estimate future needs in terms of enrollment. Unnecessary duplication of closely related types or items of supplies should be avoided. A standard list of the supplies used in the system should be adopted by the Board of Education and published. Each item should be accompanied by definite specifications and probable cost. Such list should be modified as necessity demands. Expenditures should be in accordance with budgetary provisions. *Watertown, N. Y.*, pp. 30-31.

That the school committee, both in theory and in practice, require all other members of the professional staff to report to the superintendent of schools, and that they make it clear that these persons are responsible only to the superintendent of schools and not to members of the school committee.

That the superintendent of schools be supported in his administration of the schools by a deputy superintendent as assistant superintendent in charge of elementary schools, an assistant superintendent in charge of secondary and special schools, an assistant superintendent in charge of business affairs, a director of physical education and health service, a director of research, and a director of census and attendance.

That the assistant superintendent in charge of business affairs be given direction of those problems which have to do with the erection, operation, and maintenance of school buildings, the purchase and distribution of supplies, the keeping of accounts, and the preparation of the budget.

That the director of research and vocational guidance be given an adequate staff and much more generous support to the end that he may supply to the superintendent of schools, and through him to the school committee, a basis in scientific inquiry for the recommendations upon which the committee is asked to pass.

That a director of census and attendance be appointed and that this service be much more adequately maintained. That the director of physical education and health service be selected upon the basis of his knowledge of physical education and of the medical service to be developed in the school system. *Providence, R. I.*, p. 31.

The present independence of the departments ought to be replaced by the centralization of these into one department, the educational, with sub-departments, under proper executive heads. The present independence of the School Clerk, though it works very well with the present appointee, is fundamentally wrong in principle. Schools are maintained for the sake of the educational side, and the success of affairs on the purely educational side is dependent, in no small measure on the hearty coöperation of both the School Clerk and the Superintendent of Properties. While exercising large independent jurisdiction in many matters, both should be subject to the jurisdiction of the Superintendent of Schools. He cannot, properly, be held accountable for the successful conduct of the educational affairs entrusted to him unless, in the final analysis, he has such final control. Under the present plan there are two departments, clear and distinct, when there should be but one, and that one the educational, properly subdivided for efficient administration. *Portland, Ore.*, p. 21.

The superintendent should be official head of the school system and much of the policy in the development of the school system should emanate from him; where he is so, the board should follow his judgment and leadership, and should not superimpose its own judgment, except in matters of large importance. *Butte, Mont.*, p. 113.

A waste of pay, $4,000, for an educational expert and then disregard his advice and judgment. The proper duties of a board enumerated. *Butte, Mont.*, p. 115.

The board should divest itself of routine detail and delegate such work to its employed executives. . . . The board should concern itself with getting things done and stop attempting to do so many of them itself. . . . A single-headed form of organization under the leadership of the superintendent of schools would be better than the present double-headed organization. *Butte, Mont.*, pp. 134-5.

That the Superintendent of Schools be elected for a term of from four to six years, and that he be given a legal status which he does not now enjoy, making him the chief executive officer of the Board of School Commissioners, and requiring that all assistant superintendents, supervisors, principals and teachers be elected by the Board of School Commissioners only on his nomination and recommendation. *Baltimore, Md.*, Vol. II, p. 6.

The Superintendent of Schools should be the chief executive officer of the Board of School Commissioners. *Baltimore, Md.,* Vol. II, p. 8.

It has already been pointed out that the Superintendent of Schools should be the chief executive officer of the board. This status is accepted by all competent authorities in so far as it affects the educational relationships alone. It is the opinion of the Survey Commission that this status of the superintendent of Schools should hold also with reference to all business matters connected with the school system. *Baltimore, Md.,* Vol. II, p. 24.

Recommendation that Board of Superintendents be abolished. Goodnow and Howe quoted as authority. Reasons given. *New York City,* p. 10.

The reform will be completed when the superintendent is made the chief executive officer of the School Committee as hereinbefore outlined.

The various boards which now exercise executive functions over school activities, such as the Board of Apportionment and the Salary Board, would be needless if the chief executive power rested in the superintendent.

That the superintendent of Schools be made the chief executive officer of the school committee.

That the secretary of the School Committee report to the superintendent. *Boston, Mass.,* pp. 62-64.

That the responsibility for the conduct of the school system is at the present time widely diffused among the board, committees, members of the board, secretary, superintendent, etc., is largely ascribable to the state law which does not expressly permit the superintendent of schools to be the real responsible leader of the school system. *Harrisburg, Pa.,* p. 8.

That dual executive system be established (until proper legislation can be secured by virtue of which the superintendent of schools will become the chief executive). *Harrisburg, Pa.,* p. 10.

The superintendent of schools should be the chief executive of the board in administrative and educational matters. In his office there is need of a secretary as well as stenographer. *Utica, N. Y.,* pp. 40-41.

Summary:

1. The Public School system of St. Louis is governed by a Board of Education chosen at large by the people. The powers of the Board of Education are granted to it by Charter, and in general, the Board has such corporate powers as are possessed by school districts in the State of Missouri.

2. The Charter itself makes an accurate discrimination between those duties which are essentially legislative and those which are essentially of executive character, apportioning the former to the Board and reserving the latter to the officers of the Board, subject to final ratification by the Board.

3. There are six executive officers who act as expert advisors to the Board and professional executives of the Board's acts and resolves. They derive their powers directly from the Charter. The heads of these executive departments are appointed by the Board for terms of

four years except in the case of the Auditor, whose term is two years. Their salaries are fixed by the Board, and the same may not be decreased during their term of office.

4. The Superintendent of Instruction and the Commissioners of Buildings and Supplies are made responsible for the efficient conduct of the actual work of the Board by being given full powers in relation thereto. The Secretary and Treasurer and the Attorney are held to a similar accounting so far as possible by a similar device.

5. On its executive side the School Department has no single head, but rather four distinct heads, who administer distinct separate departments, but whose work is unified in part by periodical and by occasional conferences, and in part by provisions of the Charter or provisions of the regulations, for seeing the most likely points of overlapping and waste and providing appropriate preventive measure therefor.

The organization of the School Department of the City of St. Louis is unusual and amongst the largest cities of the country unique. It is built upon a Charter which both in legal structure and in its embodiment of the best accepted principles of efficiency in school administration and government is remarkable. As a result, for a period of years longer than is necessary for a child to receive the utmost educational privileges that the city can offer, the school system has been carried on with efficiency, with harmony and dignity, rejoicing in the confidence of the people and in the respect of the other great cities of the Union. *St. Louis, Mo.*, Vol. IV, pp. 78-80.

The law should prescribe strict qualifications for superintendents, requiring them to have had a specified amount of training particularized for the work of such an officer as he seeks to become. To this may be added other desirable requisites:

The Board of Education serves its constituency best by selecting a competent executive and supporting him in his administration of the school system. The board should require of the Superintendent of Schools from time to time a report of the work which he has done. The Superintendent should present this record to the Board of Education, and should expect to demonstrate the soundness of the policies which he has advocated and to support in terms of measurable achievement his administration of schools. *Watertown, N. Y.*, p. 15.

The Superintendent of Schools should be responsible for the initiation and execution of all plans relating to the construction, operation and maintenance of the school plant. The Superintendent of Schools should be charged with the responsibility for initiating school building plans in order that the educational program shall be given precedence over all other considerations. *Watertown, N. Y.*, p. 33.

In the discussion of the work of the School Committee reference has frequently been made to the Superintendent of Schools and his staff.

Regardless of any change which may be brought about in the method of supporting the schools, or in the constitution of the School Committee, the main dependence for an efficient administration of the schools of Providence must rest with the Superintendent of Schools and his associates. If efficiency is to be secured, the Superintendent of Schools must be recognized as the chief executive officer of the School Committee and must be supported by assistants directly responsible to himself. The proposed organization of the administrative staff is given in Chart 2. (This chart shows the proper organization of the executive department of the schools.) *Providence, R. I.*, p. 27.

All executive details should be placed in the hands of this chief executive officer who should be allowed an administrative staff trained and competent to render service which is commensurate with the service demanded by any other large organization. *Stamford, Conn.*, p. 16.

That the Superintendent be made to become the real educational leader for the school system, or to give place to some one who can. To this end, he should be freed from as much detail and clerical work as is possible. *Portland, Ore.*, p. 36.

The powers of the Board of School trustees are large,—too large, in fact for any lay board of school officers to exercise intelligently, unless they obtain and follow as good expert advice as they are able to obtain. . . . The Board should have confidence in the ability and good judgment of the superintendent or replace him. They should not assume authority in educational matters. *Butte, Mont.*, pp. 112-3.

In the main, however, a city must depend on the board and the superintendent as being the expert guardian of the interests of the children. *Cleveland, Ohio*, p. 14.

Powers and Duties of City Boards of Education

The powers and duties of a city school board should be set forth in the law by the Legislature as distinctly legislative, and they might well be classified under the following general heads:

1. Prescribed powers.
2. Optional powers.
3. Denied powers, i.e., things that are expressly forbidden by the codes.

1. *Prescribed Powers.* The prescribed powers should embrace those acts properly performed by boards, and which have been so well analyzed that for the most part the best method for their performance is known. Many such functions lend themselves quite readily to standardization; and, other things being equal, they should be standardized. They should then be written into the general law as definitely prescribed powers.

The board should free itself from details of organization and administration, giving its time and attention to legislative and judicial matters. *Wilmington, Del.*, p. 27.

The right relationship between the Board of Education and Superintendent of Schools will be developed only when the members of the Board of Education cease to think of their function as having to do with the execution of the policies which they adopt; when they scrutinize carefully each proposal brought before them by the Superintendent of Schools, and having passed upon it, stand fast. *Watertown, N. Y.*, p. 19.

Evidence has been submitted showing how the board of education through its committee organization and through the functioning of these committees is actually performing many of the functions which its executives should perform, thus enabling the board to devote its time and attention to the formulation of policies. *Watertown, N. Y.*, p. 21.

The most important duty of the members of the School Committee is to select the highest type of executive that can be found. After they have chosen the superintendent of schools they are under obligation to require him to report from time to time concerning the achievements of the school system and the plans which he and his staff have to propose for the development of the school system. The superintendent of schools should be required to present his case with all of the evidence available with respect to the validity of the educational program involved, and he must be ready whenever called upon to defend in terms of measured achievement his administration. *Providence, R. I.*, p. 24.

In order to secure the best results for the school system of Stamford, a complete revision of the organization of the Board of Education should be effected and the relationship of the superintendent of schools to the School Committee should be altered. The duties of the Board of Education should become purely legislative and the administration should be so organized that the superintendent, as chief executive of the School Committee, administers the educational program which has been approved and adopted by the School Committee. The relationship of the superintendent of Schools to the School Committee may be expressed by defining the duties of the Board. The more important of the obligations which should rest upon the School Committee are as follows:

1. To choose a chief executive officer, the superintendent of schools, and to support him in the discharge of his duties.

2. To appoint, upon nomination and recommendation of the superintendent of schools, assistant superintendents, supervisors, principals and teachers.

3. To consider carefully the annual budget for maintenance of the school system, prepared by the superintendent of schools and his assistants, and to adopt it after full discussion and with such modifications as they feel are necessary.

4. To adopt, upon the recommendation of the superintendent of schools, textbooks selected and courses of study developed by the superintendent of

schools, the supervisory staff and such teachers as may be invited by them to participate in these activities.

5. To require and to discuss reports of the superintendent of schools and of his chief assistants concerning the development of the school system in terms of the achievements of pupils, teachers and supervisors.

6. To consider and to pass upon the recommendations of the superintendent of schools for additional capital outlays for buildings, sites, improvements and the like.

7. To adopt, after consultation with the superintendent of schools, a set of rules which will determine the government of the school system.

8. To act as a court of final appeal for teachers, supervisors, and school patrons in cases which the superintendent of schools or his assistants have not been able to dispose of, or which may be appealed from the decision of the superintendent of schools.'' *Stamford, Conn.*, p. 14.

The principles of good corporation organization need to be applied to educational affairs, and Boards of School Directors need to assume more the position of a Board of Directors for a large corporation, giving to their executive officers the authority which corporation Directors give to their Presidents and Superintendents. The proper functions of the Board of Directors are to supply funds, to supervise expenditure, and to determine what additions to the plant or extensions of the business are to be undertaken. So long as the business prospers the Board should leave the details of employment and management to the President and the heads of departments; when the business ceases to prosper they should either change their business methods or change their executive heads. *Portland, Ore.*, p. 26.

The President of the New York Board quoted:

The Board of Education should devote its energies to the consideration of the larger aspects of educational policy; to the appointment of those who are to carry out its policies; and to the making of those general regulations that will relieve the board from the necessary consideration of details that can be otherwise disposed of. *Cleveland, Ohio*, p. 64.

It is recommended that the Board of School Commissioners be given a larger degree of control over the money available for the public schools of the city . . . Board of education shall have general and supervisory control, government and management of the public schools . . . and to levy such taxes as are or may be authorized by law for school purposes. *Baltimore, Md.*, Vol. II, p. 10.

The following are suggested as remedies to enable the school system of Buffalo to function more efficiently.

1. There should be an absolute divorcement of all school affairs from the municipal and political affairs of the city.

2. The essential, fundamental provisions of the law regulating the school system should be incorporated into the statutes and the controlling body of the school system should be given the power to supplement these statutes through the adoption of regulations.

3. The board of education should be made the supreme local authority in the government and administration of the school system.

4. The board of education should be given the authority to appoint the superintendent of education. It should also be authorized to appoint such other officers and assistants as may be necessary for the proper administration of the school system and to appoint principals and teachers employed in the schools. These officers, assistants, principals and teachers, however, should be appointed from eligible lists, upon the nomination of the superintendent of education. The board should also be given the power of removal for misconduct or inefficiency.

5. The board of education should be given the power and authority to create such organization as may be necessary to manage, operate, supervise and maintain the school system of the city and to modify such organization from time to time as changing conditions may require.

6. The board of education should also have the power to select school sites, to approve plans and specifications for school buildings and to repair and construct school buildings.

7. Provision should be made in the law for the general maintenance of the schools by some method which will afford definite appropriations based upon the increasing needs of a school system to be maintained in a city having such progressive ideas on economic and social questions as the residents of Buffalo have shown themselves to possess. *Buffalo, N. Y.*, pp. 21-30.

2. *Optional Powers*. The optional powers would embrace all of those acts properly performed by city boards, which for one reason or another, are likely to vary from time to time in some important detail, so that any attempt to standardize their performance would result in a high degree of formalism. However, as many of these powers as can be anticipated from a study of precedents should be specified in the general law as optional with the board, for the sake of explicitness. But as unforeseen emergencies are certain to arise, a blanket control clause, carefully hedged by the phrase, "reasonably necessary and proper", should be inserted to afford temporary relief. Then as precedents are built up by boards, these acts should be either approved or disapproved by statute as optional powers.

The school board limited only by the will of the people should be able to fix the local school tax rate. This board should, in like manner, be permitted to determine how school monies should be spent without review or control by any other body. The members of such a board should be elected at large on a non-partisan separate school ballot. *Watertown, N. Y.*, p. 1.

If the State legislature considers that cities should not levy more than 10 mills, it should at least permit the electors of a city to vote whether the tax rate can be more than this amount. The people of any city can surely be trusted not to tax themselves beyond their willingness to pay and should be permitted to support as generously as they will the schools for the education of their children. *Elyria, Ohio,* p. 26.

The Survey Staff recommends that no land be purchased or improved for school buildings, no building or addition to an existing school building constructed, acquired, or appropriated for school purposes, and no furnishings installed in any building or addition to building constructed, acquired, or appropriated for school purposes, unless the location of such land, the acquisition of such building, the plans of such building or addition to a building, or such furnishings respectively shall have been recommended or approved by the School Committee. *Providence, R. I.,* p. 11.

The School Committee should insist from time to time upon having brought before it evidence of the efficiency of the school system.'' *Providence, R. I.,* p. 25.

The people of any city can surely be trusted not to tax themselves beyond their willingness to pay and should be permitted to support as generously as they will the schools for the education of their children. *Elyria, Ohio.*

It (the Board) should not only select and purchase school sites, but, under the guidance of its proper technical experts, it should plan and construct schoolhouses and make all necessary repairs to the school plant. *San Francisco, Cal.*

3. *Denied Powers.* The denied powers consist of:

a. Those denied expressly or impliedly by statutes;

b. Those denied because inconsistent with the purposes for which the city board is created;

c. Those denied by court decision as being against public policy, *ultra vires,* or for some other reason.

Lay members of a school committee should not be expected to administer or supervise the schools of Providence. *Providence, R. I.,* p. 24.

Chief function of a board of school trustees is to govern, rather than to minutely supervise. *Butte, Mont.,* p. 116.

. . . the board of school trustees is vested with large authority in the control of public education. The commission recommends that there be a clear differentiation between the legislative functions exercised by the board of school trustees and the executive powers vested by them in the superintendent of schools, and the school clerk. There can never be any adequate administration of schools without placing of large responsibility upon executive officials, chosen by the board of school trustees, and this responsibility can never be adequately met except when the board vests in the superintendent of schools authority commensurate with his responsibility. *Butte, Mont.,* p. 150.

Boards of Education exist for the purpose of getting schools managed,—not for the purpose of managing the schools themselves. Their work is to get the things done rather than to do them. When they overlook this fundamental principle, confusion results. Responsibility becomes scattered. *Cleveland, Ohio,* p. 14.

The selection of teachers is a professional function, which professional experts ought to handle. The Board of School Directors is not competent to handle such a function in the best manner, and poor results almost invariably follow their attempt to do so. . . .

The Board should also cease to give hearings to principals and supervisors, or require reports as to teachers from them. All matters relating to instruction should be referred to the Superintendent and his assistants; principals of schools should deal with them, and not with members of the Board. *Portland, Ore.,* p. 49.

Instead of examining its teachers, as is now done, it might be much wiser to rely entirely on the state or county certification and save the energy now expended in conducting a separate examination. Instead, if any examination is felt to be desirable, such could presuppose the legal certificate required by law, and be made strictly professional in character. *Portland, Ore.,* p. 51.

The board of education has given too much attention in the past to the administrative details relating to educational supervision, especially regarding the qualifications of teachers and the respective merits of textbooks. This practice was being corrected by the board even before the law of 1917 fixed responsibility for such matters. The printed rules on these matters, however, need radical revision. *Utica, N. Y.,* pp. 40-41.

The School Committee . . . must pass upon all matters which have to do with the maintenance and development of the public school system. As laymen they cannot to advantage, and should not therefore attempt to administer the school system. *Boston, Mass.,* pp. 7-8.

SUMMARY

There is no better way known to govern the schools of a city than by a board of education:

a. Consisting of 5 or 7 members;
b. Elected at large by the voters; and for a term of 5 years or more;
c. Serving gratis;
d. Without standing committees;
e. Fiscally independent;
f. Headed by an expert executive as superintendent of schools;
g. Composed of successful business and professional people willing to confine the activities of the board to legislation.

In Appendix I an attempt has been made to incorporate these fundamental legal principles into a proposed act. It is probable that school authorities and legislatures might well use that suggested act in a slightly modified form on which to construct their laws for city school districts.

CHAPTER VIII

A CHECKING LIST FOR THE LEGAL STATUS OF A CITY SCHOOL BOARD

THE ORIGIN

The checking list embodied in this chapter is a result of the findings and implications of this study. Whatever legal principles or provisions the study has indicated as good potential practice, and likely to accelerate educational progress, have been incorporated in this checking list.

The numerous principles and provisions were then organized in the present logical form and order, so as to facilitate the work of checking the laws of a given state against it.

To check a state, read the given code and check the provisions made in it on the list. By this procedure it is easy to measure, by comparison, the probable efficiency and worth of the code so checked.

CHECKING LIST

BY CHECKING THE LEGAL PRACTICES OF CITY SCHOOL BOARDS OF ANY STATE AGAINST THIS LIST IT MAY BE DETERMINED BY COMPARISON HOW CLOSELY THE STATE CHECKED CONFORMS TO WHAT THE FINDINGS OF THIS STUDY INDICATE TO BE DESIRABLE

I. Federal sanction by the Tenth Amendment—checked for all states.

II. State constitutional provisions should:
   1. Charge legislature to provide free system for *all* children.
   2. Make public support imperative.
   3. Make public control imperative.
   4. Fix scope from kindergarten to graduate school.
   5. Declare education a state function.

III. The State Legislature should:
   1. Provide for creation and later modification of school districts.
   2. Make it mandatory that these agent districts establish and maintain a system of free schools for all children of the State.
   3. Provide for the organization of the school districts:
      a. For elections for officers.
      b. For elections to determine policies.

4. Provide the district machinery for levying and collection of taxes.
5. Provide for subsequent changes of the above.
6. Provide for a Board of Education to act as agent of state and district.
7. Prescribe number of members of Board of Education.
8. Prescribe method of organization of Board of Education.
9. Fix the legal status of the Board of Education.
10. Prescribe election at large, non-partisan ballot, at independent election.
11. Prescribe qualifications of members of Board of Education.
12. Prescribe qualifications of electors.
13. Prescribe length of official term of members of Board of Education so as to secure continuity in personnel.
14. Prescribe number of members of Board of Education to be elected at each stated election.
15. Provide for filling vacancies on Board of Education.
16. Prescribe the simplest possible formality for placing names of candidates for Board of Education on non-partisan ballot.
17. Fix the fiscal year of the Board of Education.
18. Require some system of standard reports, fiscal and educational.
19. Prescribe regular meetings of the Board of Education.
20. Provide for special meetings of the Board of Education for specific purposes.
21. Provide for paid clerical help.
22. Prohibit standing committees on the Board of Education.
23. Provide for special committees for specific and single purposes.

IV. The School District should:
   1. Elect a Board of Education.
   2. Vote on general policies.
   3. Vote on certain specific policies.

V. Powers and Duties of the Board of Education:
   1. Prescribed Powers.
      a. Conduct all school elections:
         1) Prepare necessary ballots.
         2) Appoint judges of the election.
         3) Arrange for polling places.
         4) See that polling places are open during voting hours.
      b. Meet regularly each month.
      c. Hold special meetings for extraordinary needs.
      d. Reorganize at the July meeting:
         1) Elect President.
         2) Elect Vice-President.
         3) Secretary of the Board to be:
            a) In large cities—assistant superintendent in charge of business department.
            b) In small cities—head clerk of the superintendent's office.
         4) Treasurer of the Board to be the City Treasurer.

e. Elect a Superintendent as chief executive of the Board.
f. Elect, from nominations by the Superintendent:
  1) Assistant Superintendents.
  2) Principals.
  3) Supervisors.
  4) Teachers.
  5) Clerks.
  6) Janitors.
g. Fix the tenure of the above.
h. Adopt, on recommendation by the Superintendent, a salary schedule.
i. Require the Superintendent to prepare an annual budget, consider, modify and approve it:
  1) Redistribute the budget, if necessary.
  2) Keep budget within revenues.
j. Require Superintendent to submit plans for extension or modification of the scope of the school.
k. Prepare, with the Superintendent, set of rules for the government of the schools.
l. Prepare, with the Superintendent, set of by-laws for the government and regulation of the Board.
m. Require of the Superintendent an annual report showing:
  1) Financial status of the system.
  2) Results of the pupil accounting system for past year.
  3) Miscellaneous items.
n. Require the making and keeping of continuing permanent census of all children from birth to 21 years.
o. Pass on all building programs, building and architect's plans submitted and approved by the Superintendent.
p. Submit drafts of needed legislation to the State Legislature.
q. Authorize payment of all bills approved by Superintendent.
r. Authorize or conduct all necessary litigation.
s. Approve course of study proposed by Superintendent.
t. Approve purchase of texts and other supplies selected by Superintendent.
u. Approve reasonable expenditures for proper publicity for the schools.
v. Sit as court of appeal from decisions by the Superintendent.
w. Consider all communications on matters of policy.
x. Visit the schools to investigate their efficiency.
y. Require executive staff to prepare all required state and county reports, and to furnish information concerning the school system for use by the board.
z. Borrow money for operating the schools not to exceed .... per cent of the anticipated revenues for any one year.
aa. Submit matters of policy, such as bond issues, to the direct vote of the district.

bb. Establish and maintain school libraries.
cc. Establish and maintain playgrounds.
dd. Make all necessary and proper contracts.
ee. Superintend, through the executive officer, all buildings.
ff. At the request of the Superintendent, pass resolutions authorizing the performance of needful duties not otherwise authorized.
gg. Require secretary to keep minutes of all meetings.
hh. Authorize employees to be dismissed for sufficient cause.
ii. Exercise all other powers necessary and proper to the conduct of the schools.

2. Powers That Should Be Optional with City Boards of Education.

These embrace acts properly performed by city boards of education that are likely to vary from time to time as emergencies arise. As precedents are built up these acts would in time be either approved or disapproved by statute as optional powers.

3. Powers That Should Be Denied to City Boards of Education.
a. To let contracts for building without sealed bids.
b. To let contracts for building to any other than the lowest responsible bidder, board to be sole judge of responsibility.
c. To have standing committees.
d. To have special committees for other than specific tasks, the completion of which shall automatically dismiss the committees.
e. To pass on matters except as a unit.
f. To pass any independent pension regulation.
g. To fail to enforce the state pension regulations.
h. To transact business with less than a quorum present.
i. To elect a Superintendent by a vote of less than three.
j. To levy taxes in any manner not prescribed by the state legislature.
k. To levy more than the maximum taxes allowed by the state legislature.
l. To exercise any other power expressly or impliedly denied by statutes.
m. To exercise powers inconsistent with the purposes for which the city board of education is created.
n. To exercise powers denied by court decision as being against public policy, *ultra vires,* or for some other reason.

VI. The Relation of Superintendent to the City Board:
1. The chief executive officer of the Board.
2. Elected first for a short probationary term.
3. Subsequent elections for long terms.
4. Mandatory that board elect a thoroughly trained superintendent.
5. Through the rules of the board, the superintendent should be required to organize and utilize an executive staff or cabinet.

VII. The General School Law should apply in all cases not provided for by specific enactments.

APPENDIX I

A SUGGESTED ACT

The following proposed act may be considered as:

1. A compilation of the best practices of the present day.
2. A composite of the objectives of current trends in the theory of school legislation, as set forth in the several city school surveys and other literature bearing on the subject.
3. The embodiment of the recommendations resulting from this study of the legal status of city school boards.

AN ACT for the Creation and Maintenance of City School Districts, prescribing their Form of Organization, the Powers and Duties of the Districts and of their Lawfully Constituted Boards of Education.

Section 1. Each city of the State of ...., as now organized, or as it may be later organized, together with whatever adjacent territory is, or may legally become a part thereof, shall constitute a city school district under the name of, "The (*name of city*) City School District", and shall be governed under the provisions of this act, as follows:

Section 2. All legislative powers herein granted to the districts shall be vested in a Board of Education, which shall consist of five members, each of whom shall be regularly elected for a term of five years, by and from the qualified electors of the districts; they shall be chosen from the district at large, and on a nonpartisan ballot; and they shall receive no compensation for their services.

When vacancies occur from any cause whatsoever, the remaining members of the Board of Education shall choose a qualified person who shall hold office until the next annual school election, at which time a member shall be regularly elected to fill the unexpired term.

The incumbent Board of Education shall conduct all school elections; they shall prepare the necessary ballots; appoint the requisite number of judges of election; arrange for sufficient polling places; and, see that they are open for balloting from 1:00 P.M. to 6:00 P.M. on the third Tuesday of May, which shall be the date of the annual school election.

Members of the Board of Education in office at the time of the enactment of this law shall constitute, in whole or in part, the new Board of Education, and each such member shall continue to serve for the time for which he was formerly chosen; but, no board shall consist of less than five members.

As the terms of members of Boards of Education in office at the time of the enactment of this law shall expire, it shall be so arranged, in order to secure continuity of educational policy for the district, that the term of one member shall regularly expire each year.

Section 3. The Board of Education shall meet regularly each month and at the July meeting the members, or members-elect shall subscribe to and file the oath of office with the secretary of the board. Immediately thereafter the board shall reorganize by electing one of its members as president and another as vice-president of the board. The assistant superintendent of the schools who is in charge of the business department, shall be ex-officio secretary to the board; and in the smaller cities which do not employ assistant superintendents, the head clerk of the superintendent's office shall act as secretary; and the city treasurer shall be treasurer for the Board of Education. In all cases these officers shall perform the usual functions of such officials.

Special meetings may be called from time to time, but only in cases of extraordinary need thereof, and then to consider only such matters as were specified in the notice of the special meeting.

Section 4. Boards of Education in City Districts shall have power and it shall be their duty:

1. To elect a superintendent as chief executive of the board and in accordance with the provisions of this act, fix his salary and assign his duties.

2. To require the superintendent to prepare, in conjunction with his associates, the annual budget, based upon a suitable cost accounting system of the past year and an estimate of new needs for the coming year, and distributed in sufficient detail as it is proposed to expend it, probably under the heads of:

a.	General control	approximating	4%
b.	Instructional service	"	65%
c.	Operation of the plant	"	10%
d.	Debt service	"	7%
e.	Fixed charges	"	2%
f.	Capital outlay	"	6%
g.	Auxiliary	"	2%
h.	Miscellaneous	"	4%

The board shall then duly consider the budget and approve it as proposed or as they may finally modify it; but they shall always consider capital outlay separately when it exceeds 10%, or when new buildings are proposed.

The Board shall exercise due care that the budget total does not exceed the maximum amount of legal revenues, but should this excess occur, the board shall have power to redistribute the actual revenues in whatever way they may deem most equitable; and, upon adoption of the budget, the total amount thereof, without review of any other official or body of officials, shall be spread upon the tax rolls, and the revenues therefrom shall be expended as the Board of Education directs.

3. To require the superintendent of schools to submit, from time to time for their consideration, plans prepared in conjunction with his cabinet, for

the extension or modification of the scope of the school, in any or all of the following particulars:

1) Kindergartens.
2) Elementary schools.
3) Junior high schools.
4) Senior high schools.
5) Vocational schools.
6) Continuation schools.
7) Any other special schools.
8) Health program.
9) Extra-curricular activities.
10) Other proposals for extending the school service.

4. To appoint from those nominated by the superintendent, all assistant superintendents, principals, supervisors, teachers, clerks, janitors, and other employees.

5. To adopt, in conjunction with the superintendent, a salary schedule for assistant superintendents, principals, supervisors, teachers, clerks, janitors and other employees; and, to fix the tenure of any or all of these.

6. To prepare in conjunction with the superintendent of schools:

a. A set of rules for the government and regulation of the schools.

b. A set of by-laws for the government and regulation of the board.

7. To require the superintendent to prepare, in conjunction with his associates for the board's adoption, an annual report of the schools, including a full statement of:

a. The financial status of the system.

b. A summary of the results of the pupil accounting system for the past year.

c. Miscellaneous items.

8. To require the executive officer in charge of attendance to make and keep a permanent continuing census of all children of the district from birth to the age of twenty-one.

9. To consider and pass upon all building programs, building and architect's plans, submitted and approved by the superintendent of schools.

10. To submit drafts of needed general legislation to the state legislature.

11. To authorize the payment of all bills which have the approval of the superintendent.

12. To authorize or conduct all necessary litigation.

13. To approve the course of study proposed by the executive and his cabinet.

14. To approve and purchase texts and other supplies selected by the executive and his cabinet.

15. To approve reasonable expenditures for proper publicity for the schools; and uphold the policies adopted as a board.

16. To sit as a court to consider vital matters when appealed to them from the decisions of the chief executive by assistant superintendents, principals, teachers, employees or parents.

17. To receive and consider all communications on matters of policy.

18. To visit the schools, officially, to investigate their efficiency, upon invitation of the executive staff or of the teaching force.

19. To require the executive staff to prepare all state and county reports required by law; and to furnish from time to time, for use by the board, information on the state of affairs throughout the school system.

20. To borrow money for operating the schools, on the credit of the district, not exceeding — per cent of the anticipated revenues for any one year.

21. To submit proposals to bond the district, and other questions of finance and school policy to a direct vote of the district.

22. To establish and maintain school libraries.

23. To establish and maintain playgrounds, throughout the year.

24. To make all necessary and proper contracts including the purchase of property.

25. To superintend through the executive officer all buildings.

26. To pass resolutions at the request of the superintendent, authorizing him, or the executive staff, to perform needful duties not otherwise authorized.

27. To require the secretary to keep stenographic minutes of all meetings.

28. To authorize employees to be dismissed for sufficient cause.

29. To exercise all other powers which are necessary and proper for carrying out the provisions of this act.

Section 5.

1. No board shall let contracts for building except on sealed bids for same, and they shall let all such contracts to the lowest responsible bidder; the board shall be the sole judge of such responsibilities.

2. No board shall have standing committees nor special committees except for specific tasks, the completion of which shall automatically dismiss the committee.

3. No action shall be binding on the district unless passed when the board acted as a unit.

4. No city board of education may pass any independent pension regulation, but they must enforce that of the state.

5. No board shall transact business unless there is present a quorum of three members, and a vote of three shall always be necessary to elect a superintendent.

6. No board shall levy taxes in any other manner than that prescribed by the legislature; and only within the maximum limit set thereby.

Section 6. The Executive Power.

1. The executive power of the district and of the Board of Education herein granted shall be vested in a superintendent of schools who shall be elected by the Board of Education, for terms as follows: When first elected each superintendent of schools shall be elected for a term of one year; thereafter, for terms of five years; but, the Board may cancel its contract with him to become effective on July 1st of any year provided that he be notified of such intention not later than May 1st.

2. No person shall be eligible to the office of superintendent of schools of any city who does not have a Bachelor's and a Master's degree from some standard college or university, and have included in the training at least 30 semester hours of professional education; provided, however, that superintendents of schools in cities at the time of the enactment of this law may be reëlected for one full five year term before being required to conform to the above requirements.

3. The superintendent of schools shall organize a cabinet to assist and advise him in the work of administration of the schools. All assistant superintendents shall be members; and, there shall be one or more representatives elected from each of the following groups: Principals, supervisors, and teachers. The cabinet shall perform the duties herein delegated to it: it shall perform the usual duties of an executive department; and such other duties as the superintendent of schools shall direct.

4. The executive department under the direction of the superintendent of schools shall manage all school property; purchase supplies authorized by the board of education; administer the schools; direct the supervision of instruction; execute the orders of the board; and, in conjunction with the civil authorities, enforce the school law, and law relating to children of school age. They shall be especially charged with enforcement of the compulsory education law.

Section 7. The boards of education for city districts shall, in all matters not specifically provided for in this act, be controlled and subject to the general school laws of the state; provided, however, that all acts or parts of acts in conflict with any of the provisions of this act are hereby repealed, in so far as they relate to city districts.

APPENDIX II

GLOSSARY OF UNUSUAL LEGAL TERMS, ABBREVIATIONS, AND EXPLANATORY NOTES

Agency, one person legally acting for another.

A. L. R., American Law Reports.

Am., American.

App., appeal.

Apriori, from what went before.

A. S. R., American State Reports.

Atl., Atlantic.

Body corporate, a group having powers of a corporation.

Bona fide, in good faith.

Cas., cases.

Civ., civil.

Code, a law or section of laws.

Codification, arranging in codes.

Common Law, the old English law brought together in the reign of Edward the Confessor.

Corporation, an artificial person at law; a body chartered or incorporated by the state.

Corpus Juris, an encyclopedia of law.

Ct., court.

D. C., District of Columbia.

Declaratory, expressing.

De facto, in fact, or from the fact.

De jure, by legal right.

E., east, eastern.

Enc., encyclopedia of law and procedure.

Fed., federal.

Legal entity, a person, natural or artificial, recognized at law.

Loco parentis, in place of the parents.

L. R. A., Lawyers' Reports Annotated.

Mandatory, obligatory.

Met., Metcalf.

N., northwest.

N. S., new series.

Pac., Pacific.

Pick., Pickering.

Public Policy, the rightful interests of the public.

Quasi, having part of the attributes.

R. C. L., Ruling Case Law, a cyclopedic legal work.

Rep., reporter, encyclopedic reports of cases tried. Reporters and reports of decisions are made in law in the following ways:
Doe v. Roe, 22 Cal. 141, would mean the 22d vol. of the California State reports, page 141. This same case might be reported in the Pacific Reporter thus: Doe v. Roe, 14 Pac. 120, and would mean that this case is reported in the 14th vol. on page 120. Cross references, i.e., when one case is looked up and other cases are wanted to support it, may be found in such legal works as Lawyers' Reports Annotated.

Rt., reports, official records of trials and adjudicated cases.

S., south.

Solon, The Lawgiver of Athens.

Stare Decisis, by precedent, or formerly decided.

Sup., supreme.

Ultra vires, beyond the legal powers.

U. S., the United States.

Usurper, one exercising powers without legal right.

Void *ab initio,* illegal and not enforceable from the beginning.

V., versus or against.

APPENDIX III

REFERENCE NOTES

Chapter I

1. Cubberley, E. P. *Educational Review,* April, 1924, p. 200.

2. *A Manual of Educational Legislation,* U. S. Department of Education, Bulletin 1919, Number 4.

Chapter II

1. Board of Improvement v. Little Rock Ark. Dist., 56 Ark. 354, 19 S. W. 969, 35 A. S. R. 108, 16 L. R. A. 418; State v. Hine, 59 Conn. 50, 21 Atl. 1024, 10 L. R. A. 83; State v. Haworth, 122 Ind. 462, 23 N. E. 946, 7 L. R. A. 240; Chambers v. State, 127 Ind. 365, 26 N. E. 893, 11 L. R. A. 613; Stone v. Fritts, 169 Ind. 361, 82 N. E. 792, 14 Ann. Cas. 295, 15 L. R. A. (N. S.) 1147; State v. Freeman, 61 Kan. 90, 58 Pac. 959, 47 L. R. A. 67. Associated Schools etc. v. Rennville County School District No. 83, 122 Munn. 254, 142 N. W. 325, 47 L. R. A. (N. S.) 200. Edmondson v. Board of Education, 108 Fenn. 557, 69 S. W. 274, 58 L. R. A. 170, 24 S. E. 544, 57 A. S. R. 847, 32 L. R. A. 413.

2. Atty. Gen. v. Lowrey, 199 U. S. 233, 26 S. Ct. 27, 50 U. S. (L. ed.) 167. Pearson v. State, 56 Ark. 148, 19 S. W. 499, 35 A. S. R. 91. Freel v. Crawfordsville School City, 142 Ind. 27, N. E. 312, 37 L. R. A. 301. Kuhn v. Board of Education, 175 Mich. 438, 141 N. W. 574, 45 L. R. A. (N. S.) 972. Pittsburgh v. Sterrett Sub. District School, 204 Pa. St. 635, 54 Atl. 436, 61 L.R.A. 183. Howard v. Tacoma School Dist., 88 Wash. 167, 152 Pac. 1004, Ann. Cas. 1917D792.

3. Hassett v. Carroll, 85 Conn. 23, 81 Atl. 1013, Ann. Cas. 1913A333. Kuhn v. Board of Education, 175 Mich. 438, 141 N. W. 574, 45 L. R. A. (N. S.) 972. Crawford v. Klamath County School District No. 7, 68 Ore. 388, 137 Pac. 217, Ann. Cas. 1915C477, 50 L. R. A. (N. S.) 147, Honaker v. Board of Education, 42 W. Va., 170, 24 S. E. 544, 57 A. S. R. 847, 32 L. R. A. 413, Herald v. Board of Education, 65 W. Va. 765, 65 S. E. 102, 31 L. R. A. (N. S.) 588. School Dist. No. 56 v. St. Joseph, etc., Ins. Co., 103 U. S. 707, 26 U. S. (L. ed) 601. Doon Tp. v. Cummins, 142 U. S. 366, 12 S. Ct. 220, 35 U. S. (L. ed.) 1044. Board of Education v. DeKay, 148 U. S. 591, 13 S. Ct. 706, 37 U. S. (L. ed.) 573. Pass. School Dist. v. Hollywood City School Dist., 156 Cal. 416, 105 Pac. 122, 20 Ann. Cas. 87, 26 L. R. A. (N. S.) 485. Pasadena School Dist. v. Pasadena, 166 Cal. 7, 134 Pac. 985, Ann. Cas. 1915B1039, 47 L. R. A. (N. S.) 892. Hassett v. Carroll, 85 Conn. 23, 81 Atl. 1013, Ann. Cas 1913A333. People v. Board of Education, 101 Ill. 308, 40 Am. Rep. 196. Monticello School Town v. Kendall, 72 Ind. 91, 37 Am. Rep. 139. Andrews v. Estes, 11 Me. 267, 26 Am.

Dec. 521. Gaskell v. Dudley, 6 Metc. (Mass.) 546, 39 Am. Dec. 750. Hill v. Boston, 122 Mass. 334, 23 Am. Rep. 332. Marathon Tp. School Dist. No. 4 v. Gage, 39 Mich. 484, 33 Am. Rep. 421. Connell v. Woodard, 5 How. Miss. 665, 37 Am. Dec. 173. Fans v. Young, 30 Neb. 360, 46 N. W. 528, 27 A. S. R. 412. Smith v. Robersonville Graded School, 141 N. C. 143, 53 S. E. 524, 8 Ann. Cas. 529. Finch v. Board of Education, 30 Ohio St. 37, 27 Am. Rep. 414. Pittsburgh v. Sterrett Subdistrict School, 204 Pa. St. 635, 54 Atl. 463, 61 L. R. A. 183. Crabb v. Celeste School Dist., 105 Tex. 194, 146 S. W. 528, Ann. Cas. 1915B1146, 39 L. R. A. (N. S.) 601. Howard v. Tacoma School Dist., 88 Wash. 167, 152 Pac. 1004, Ann. Cas. 1917D792. Honaker v. Board of Education, 42 W. Va. 170, 24 S. E. 544, 57 A. S. R. 847, 32 L. R. A. 413. Herald v. Board of Education, 56 W. Va. 765, 65 S. E. 102, 31 L. R. A. (N. S.) 588, 51 A. S. R. 120, 17 Ann. Cas. 511. Freel v. Crawfordsville School City, 142 Ind. 27, 41 N. E. 312, 37 L. R. A. 301. Daniels v. Board of Education, 191 Mich. 339, 158 N. W. 23, L. R. A. 1916F468.

4. Atty. Gen. v. Lowrey, 199 U. S. 233, 26 S. Ct. 27, 50 U. S. (L. ed.) 167. Pearson v. State, 56 Ark. 148, 19 S. W. 499, 35 A. S. R. 91; Pass. School Dist. v. Hollywood School Dist., 156 Cal. 416, 105 Pac. 122, 20 Ann. Cas. 87, 26 L. R. A. (N. S.) 485; Winona v. School Dist. No. 82, 40 Minn. 13, 41 N. W. 539, 12 A. S. R. 687, 3 L. R. A. 46. Edmondson v. Board of Education, 108 Tenn. 557, 69 S. W. 274, 58 L. R. A. 170.

5. State v. Hine, 59 Conn. 50, 21 Atl. 1024, 10 L. R. A. 83. State v. Freeman, 61 Kan. 90, 58 Pac. 959, 47 L. R. A. 67. Harris v. Burr, 32 Ore. 348, 52 Pac. 17, 39 L. R. A. 768. Munsinger v. Rau, 236 Pa. 327, 84 Atl. 902, Ann. Cas. 1913E1324.

6. *Supra,* note 5.

7. *Supra,* note 5.

8. *Supra,* note 5.

9. *Supra,* note 5.

10. Ballou, Frank W. *The Appointment of Teachers in Cities,* pp. 1-130. Harvard University Press, 1915. Deffenbaugh, W. S. *School Administration in the Smaller Cities.* Bureau of Education Bulletin, 1915, No. 44.

11. Cubberley, E. P. *Public School Administration,* p. 93. Houghton Mifflin Co., Rev. ed., 1922.

12. *Supra,* note 11, pp. 90, 92.

13. *Supra,* note 10, p. 9.

14. *Supra,* note 11, p. 92; also, note 10, pp. 9-11.

15. Strayer, George D., et al. *Report of the Survey of Certain Aspects of the Public School System of Providence, R. I.,* p. 15. Oxford Press.

16. Ruling Case Law, 22:406; 24:571-572; L. R. A. n. s. 212.

17. *Supra,* note 16.

18. *Supra,* note 16.

19. Trustees of Schools v. People, 87 Ill. 303, 29 Am. Rt. 55. McCormick v. Burt, 95 Ill. 263, 35 Am. Rt. 163. State v. Webber, 108 Ind. 31, 8 N. E. 708, 58 Am. Rt. 30. Fertich v. Michener, 111 Ind. 472, 11 N. E. 605; 14

N. E. 68, 60 Am. Rt. 709. Board of Education v. Booth, 110 Ky. 53, 62 S. W. 872, 53 L. R. A. 787. Dritt v. Snodgrass, 66 Mo. 286, 27 Am. Rt. 343. King v. Jefferson City School Board, 71 Mo. 628, 36 Am. Rt. 499; McCortle v. Bates, 29 Ohio St. 419, 23 Am. Rt. 758. Ferriter v. Tyler, 48 Vt. 444, 21 Am. Rt. 133. Morrow v. Wood, 35 Wis. 59, 17 Am. Rt. 471; State v. School District No. 1 District Board, 135 Wis. 619, 116 N. W. 232, 128 A. S. R. 1050, 16 L. R. A. (N. S.) 730.

20. Atchison v. Board of Education v. DeKay, 148 U. S. 591, 13 S. Ct. 706, 37 U. S. (L. ed.) 573; Metz v. Anderson, 23 Ill. 463, 76 Am. Dec. 704, Ann. Cas. 1913E171.

21. State v. Freeman, 61 Kan. 90, 58 Pac. 959, 47 L. R. A. 67; Smith v. Simmons, 129 Ky. 93, 110 S. W. 336, 130 A. S. R. 426; Wilkinson v. Lord, 85 Neb. 136, 122 N. W. 399, 24 L. R. A. n. s. 1104.

22. Atchison et al. R. Co. v. State, 28 Okla. 94, 113 Pac. 921, 40 L. R. A. n. s. 1; Minsinger v. Raw, 236 Pa. St. 327, 84 Atl. 902, Ann. Cas. 1913C1324; School District 21 v. Fremont Co., 15 Wyo. 73, 86 Pac. 24, 11 Ann. Cas. 1058; Associated Schools of Independent Districts No. 63 v. School District No. 83, 122 Minn. 254, 142 N. W. 325, 47 L. R. A. n. s. 200; Smith v. Robersonville Graded School, 141 N. C. 143, 53 S. E. 524, 8 Ann. Cas. 529.

23. Fertich v. Michener, 111 Ind. 472, 11 N. E. 605, 14 N. E. 68, 60 Am. Rt. 709; Guernsey v. Pitkin, 32 Vt. 224, 76 Am. Dec. 171; State v. School District No. 1 Dist. Board, 135 Wis. 619, 116 N. W. 232, 128 A. S. R. 1050, 16 L. R. A. n. s. 730.

24. Erskine, John. *The Bookman,* Sept., 1924.

Chapter III

1. Dartmouth College v. Woodward, 4 Wheat (U. S.) 518, 4 (L. ed.) 629, 1 Cummings Cas. Priv. Corp. 490, W. D. Smith Cas. Corp. 148, Shep. Corp. Cas. 248. For others, see 10 Cyclopedia of Law 143.

2. State v. Standard Oil Co., 49 Ohio St. 137, 30 N. E. 279, 15 L. R. A. 145, 34 Am. St. Rep. 541; People v. North River Sugar Refining Co., 121 N. Y. 582, 24 N. E. 834, 9 L. R. A. 33; People v. Kingston M Turnpike Rd. Co., 23 Wend (N. Y.) 195, 35 Am. Dec. 551. First Nat. Bank of Chicago v. Trebein Co., 59 Ohio State 316, 52 N. E. 834.

3. People v. Assessors Village of Watertown, 1 Hill (N. Y.) 620; also, same as note 7.

4. Thomas v. Dakin, 22 Wend (N. Y.) 9.

5. Wheelack v. Mouton, 15 Vt. 519, 1 Cumming Cas. Priv. Corp. 35; Baldun v. Canfield, 26 Minn. 43, 1 N. W. 261. Parker v. Hotel Co., 96 Tenn. 252, 34 S. W. 209, 31 L. R. A. 706; Humphreys v. McKissock, 140 U. S. 304, 11 Sup. Ct. 779, 35 (L. ed.) 473; Sellers v. Greer, 172 Ill. 549, 50 N. E. 246, 40 L. R. A. 589.

6. *Infra,* note 9.

7. Pope v. Brandon, 2 Stew (Ala) 401, 66 Am. Dec. 165; Gordon v. Preston, 26 Am. Dec. 75.

8. See tables of powers and duties Chap. VI, "Relatives, nepotism restricted or prohibited." Ariz., Miss., Neb., O., 1901, etc.

9. Clark, Wm. L. *Private Corporations,* p. 8, West Publishing Co., St. Paul, Minn.

10. Stowe v. Flagg, 72 Ill. 397. Medical Inst. v. Patterson, 1 Denio (N. Y.) 61. Myers v. Manhattan Bank, 20 Ohio 283. McKim v. Odom, 3 Bland (Md.) 407, 416.

11. 1 Cumming, Cas. Priv. Corp. 148, W. D. Smith, Cas. Corp. 129, Shep. Cas. Corp. 75; Colman v. Railway Co., 10 Beav. 1, 1 Cumming, Cas. Priv. Corp. 136; Thomas v. Railroad Co., 101 U. S. 71, 25 (L. ed.) 950, 1 Cumming, Cas. Priv. Corp. 164, W. D. Smith, Cas. Corp. 132, Shep. Cas. Corp. 70; Byrne v. Manufacturing Co., 65 Conn. 336, 31 Atl. 833, 28 L. R. A. 304. State v. Lincoln Trust Co., 144 Mo. 562, 46 S. W. 593; Franklin Nat. Bank v. Whitehead, 149 Ind. 560, 49 N. E. 592, 39 L. R. A. 725, 63 Am. St. Rep. 303; Best Brewing Co. v. Klassen, 185 Ill. 37, 57 N. E. 20, 50 L. R. A. 765, 76 Am. St. Rep. 26; Bankers Union of the World v. Crawford, 67 Kan. 449, 73 Pac. 79, 100 Am. St. Rep. 465; Cumberland Tel. and Tel. Co. v. City of Evansville (C.C.), 127 Fed. 187.

12. *Infra,* note 16.

13. 1 Bl. Comm. 475, Warner v. Beers, 23 Wend. (N. Y.) 103, George, Partnerships, pp. 102-257.

14. S. P. R. Co. v. Orton (C.C.), 32 Fed. 457, 473. *Note.* In South Carolina Board Members are free from poll and road taxes and have free passage over all ferries.

15. Andrews Bros. v. Youngstown Coke Co., 86 Fed. 585, 30 C. C. A. 293. Trustees of Schools v. Tatmen, 13 Ill. 27. Bradley v. Case Scam (Ill.) 585. Mobile School Commissioners v. Putnam, 44 Ala. 506. Head v. Univ. of Mo., 47 Mo. 220.

16. Munn v. Commission Co., 15 Johns (N. Y.) 52, 8 Am. Dec. 219.

Chapter IV

1. *Black's Law Dictionary,* 2nd ed., p. 1058.

2. East Anglian Rys. Co. v. Eastern Counties Ry. Co., 11 C. B. 775, 1 Cumming, Cas. Priv. Corp. 142. Directors, etc., of Ashbury Railway Carriage and Iron Co. v. Riche, L. R., 7 H. L. 653, 1 Cumming, Cas. Priv. Corp. 152; Central Transp. Co. v. Pullman Palace Car Co., 139 U. S. 24, 11 Sup. Ct. 478, 35 (L. ed.) 55; Pittsburgh, C. & St. L. Ry. Co. v. Keokuk & H. Bridge Co., 131 U. S. 371, 9 Sup. Ct. 770, 33 (L. ed.) 157. *See also* Union Pac. Ry. Co. v. Chicago, M. & St. P. Ry. Co., 163 U. S. 564, 16 Sup. Ct. 1173, 41 (L. ed). 265; McCormich v. Bank, 165 U. S. 538, 17 Sup. Ct. 433, 41 (L. ed.) 817; California Nat. Bank v. Kennedy, 167 U. S. 362, 17 Sup. Ct. 831, 42 (L. ed.) 198; De LaVergne R. M. Co. v. German Sav. Inst., 175 U. S. 40, 20 Sup. Ct. 20, 44 (L. ed.) 65; Anglo-American Land, M. & A. Co. v. Lombard, 132 Fed. 721, 68 C. C. A. 89. Perkins v. Newark, etc., 161 Fed. 767; Rockland County v. Grear, 57 Misc. Rep. (N. Y.) 472. School District v. Stough, 4 Neb. 357; Davis v. Board, etc., 38 W. Va. 382, 18 S. E. 588. Capital Bank v. School District, etc., 63 Fed. 938; Capital Bank v. School District, etc., 1 N. D. 479, 48 N. W. 363; Turney v. Bridgeport, 55 Conn. 412, 12 Atl. 520; Wilson v. School District, etc.,

32 N. H. 118; School District, etc. v. Western Tube Co., 5 Wyo. 185, 33 Pac. 922. Gehling v. School District, etc., 10 Neb. 239, 4 N. W. 1023.

3. School District, et al. v. Currier, 45 N. H. 573.

4. State *ex rel.* Atty. Gen. v. Vickers, 58 Ohio 730.

5. Butler v. Regents of University, 32 Wis. 131.

6. Wilson v. Salamanca, 99 U. S. 501.

7. Van Sickle v. Board, Md. case 1910.

8. Louisiana, Governor Commissions the members. See La. School Codes, 1901, 1911, 1921.

9. School District, etc. v. Bennett, 52 Ark. 511, 13 S. W. 132. State v. Stewart, 90 Kan. 778, 135 Pac. 1182. Owens v. O'Brien, 78 Va. 116; Smith v. Reppard, 69 W. Va. 211, 71 S. E. 115. Jewett v. Matteson, 148 Ky. 820, 147 S. W. 924.

10. Kentucky requires members to be 30 years old. See Ky. School Codes, 1901, 1911, 1921.

CHAPTER V

1. *Black's Law Dictionary,* 2nd ed., p. 700.

2. Cooley's *Blackstone,* 3rd ed., I: 44, sec. II.

3. Cooley's *Blackstone,* 3rd ed., I: 47, sec. II.

4. Bl. Comm., Kent, I: 30.

5. *Ibid.,* note 2 and 3, I: 53.

6. *Plutarch's Lives,* Translated by J. and W. Langhorne, S. Campbell, Publisher, I: 227.

7. I Bl. Comm. 150; 2 Kent, Comm. 189.

8. Morse v. Welton, 6 Conn. 547, 16 Am. Dec. 73. Abbott v. Converse, 4 Allen (Mass) 533. Lord v. Poor, 23 Me. 569. Johnson v. Terry, 34 Conn. 259.

9. TIFFANY, W. C., *Law of Persons and Domestic Relations;* 2d ed., West Pub. Co., St. Paul, p. 259.

10. Reading v. Wilson, 38 N. J. Eq. 446; Preble v. Longfellow, 48 Me. 279, 77 Am. Dec. 227; Roscoe v. McDonald, 101 Mich. 313, 59 N. W. 603.

11. Errant v. Barlow, 14 Ves. 202; Ex Parte Mountfort, 15 Ves. 449; Clark v. Montgomery, 23 Barb. N. Y. 464; Beasley v. Watson, 41 Ala. 234; Waldron v. 76 Ala. 285. State v. Martin, 18 Mo. App. 468; Newport v. Cook, 2 Ashm. (Pa) 332.

12. Call v. Ward, 4 Watts & S. (Pa.) 118, 39 Am. Dec. 64; Edmunds Barnum v. Frost's Adm's, 17 Grat. (Va.) 398; Pinnell v. Hinkle, 54 W. Va. 119, 46 S. E. 171; Nicholson v. Spencer, 11 Ga. 607. (There are many other cases corroborating this position.)

13. SMITH, ADAM, *Wealth of Nations,* Vol. I, Ch. X, p. 2.

14. GIBBIN, H. DE B., *Industry in England,* pp. 260-3. CUNNINGHAM, W., *Growth of English Industry and Commerce,* pp. 537-41. REEVE, *History of the English Law,* Vol. III, pp. 591-600.

15. SCOTT, J. F., *Historical Essays on Apprenticeship and Vocational Education,* p. 61.

16. CUBBERLEY, E. P., *Public Education in the United States,* pp. 16-17.

17. *Ibid.*, pp. 17-18.

18. *Ibid.*, p. 22.

19. Statutes of Virginia (Hening), I: 260, 336-337; II: 298. Col. Rec. N. C., I: 448, 577-8; I: 266-7.

20. CUBBERLEY, E. P., *Public Education in the United States*, p. 22.

21. Message from the Governor Relative to Financing Education in Cities with Report of Special Commission Appointed to Study the Subject, p. 22 *et seq.*

22. VOORHEES, H. C., *The Law of the Public School System of the United States*, p. 3, note 4.

23. *A Manual of Educational Legislation*, U. S. Department of Education, Bulletin, 1919, No. 4.

24. *A Manual of Educational Legislation*, U. S. Department of Education, Bulletin, 1924, No. 36.

25. FINEGAN, THOMAS E., *Eighth Annual Report of Education Department*, No. 50, 1912; pp. 20-21, Albany, N. Y.

CHAPTER VII

1. VOORHEES, H. C., *The Law of the Public School System of the United States*, pp. 3-4. Little, Brown and Company, 1916, Boston.

2. SANDS, *The Harrisburg School Survey*, p. 35.

SURVEYS

BALTIMORE, MD. *Report of the Survey of the Public School System of Baltimore, Maryland.* G. D. Strayer, Director.

BOISE, IDAHO. *The Boise Survey: The Complete Study of the Administration of a City School System.* J. B. Sears, assisted by W. M. Proctor and J. H. Williams. World Book Co.

BOSTON, MASS. *Report of a Study of Certain Phases of the Public School System of Boston, Massachusetts.* Made under the auspices of the Finance Commission. J. H. Van Sickle. 1916.

BUFFALO, N. Y. *Examination of the Public School System of the City of Buffalo.* Educational Department of the State of New York, University of the State of New York. 1916.

BUTTE, MONT. *Report of a Survey of the School System of Butte, Montana.* Submitted to the Board of School Trustees, June 2, 1914. G. D. Strayer, Director of the Survey.

CLEVELAND, OHIO. *Cleveland Educational Survey: School Organization and Administration.* Leonard P. Ayres and others. 1916.

DENVER, COLO. *Report of the School Survey of District No. 1 in the City and County of Denver.* The School Survey Committee, Denver, Colo. 1916.

ELYRIA, OHIO. *Educational Survey of Elyria, Ohio.* Made under the direction of the U. S. Commissioner of Education. U. S. Bureau of Education Bulletin. 1918, No. 15.

EL PASO, TEXAS. *Educational Survey of the City Schools of El Paso, Texas.* P. W. Horn. Publication of the El Paso Public Schools, 1922, No. 1.

GRAND RAPIDS, MICH. *School Survey.* Board of Education, Grand Rapids, Michigan. 1916.

HACKENSACK, N. J. *Report of the Survey of the Public School System of Hackensack, New Jersey.* G. D. Strayer and N. L. Engelhardt.

HARRISBURG, PA. *School Building Survey and School Building Program.* Thomas E. Finegan, N. L. Engelhardt, and H. Perkins.

JANESVILLE, WIS. *An Educational Survey of Janesville, Wisconsin.* State Department of Public Instruction, Madison, Wis. 1915.

LEAVENWORTH, KAN. *Report of a Survey of the Public Schools of Leavenworth, Kansas.* State Normal School, Emporia, Kans. 1915.

LOCKPORT, N. Y. *A report of the Survey of the Lockport School System.* State Department of Education, The University of the State of New York. Bulletin No. 809.

MARION, ILL. *A Survey of the City Schools of Marion, Illinois.* Walter S. Monroe, Director. The University of Illinois. 1924.

MEMPHIS, TENN. *Report of a Survey of the Public School System of Memphis, Tennessee.* Made under the Direction of the Commissioner of Education. U. S. Bureau of Education. 1920.

NEW YORK CITY. *School Efficiency.* A Constructive Study Applied to New York City, Being a Summary and Interpretation of the Report on the Educational Aspects of the School Inquiry. Paul H. Hanus. World Book Co. 1913.

NIAGARA FALLS, N. Y. *A Report of the Survey of the Niagara Falls School System.* State Department of Education. the University of the State of N. Y. 1921.

PORTLAND, ORE. *The Portland Survey: a Textbook on City School Administration Based on a Concrete Study.* E. P. Cubberley, assisted by Fletcher B. Dressler and others. World Book Co. 1916.

PROVIDENCE, R. I. *Report of the Survey of Certain Aspects of the Public School System of Providence, Rhode Island.* 1923-24. Made by the Division of Field Studies, Institute of Educational Research, Teachers College, Columbia University. G. D. Strayer, Director and N. L. Engelhardt, M. B. Hillegas, J. F. Williams and J. R. McGaughy, Associate Directors.

SAN FRANCISCO, CALIF. *The Public School System of San Francisco, California.* A Report to the San Francisco Board of Education of a Survey made under the direction of the United States Commissioner of Education. U. S. Bureau of Education, Bulletin, 1917, No. 46.

SALT LAKE CITY, UTAH. *Report of the Survey of the Public School System of Salt Lake City, Utah.* 1915.

SOUTH BEND, IND. *The Public Schools of South Bend, Indiana.* Biennial Report of Board of Education, 1912-14, and School Survey by Department of Education, University of Chicago. J. F. Bobbitt.

ST. PAUL, MINN. *Report of the Survey of the School System of St. Paul, Minnesota.* Survey Commission.

ST. LOUIS, MO. *Survey of the St. Louis Public Schools.* Charles H. Judd, assisted by J. F. Bobbitt, J. B. Gragin, F. H. Daniels and others. World Book Co. 1918.

STAMFORD, CONN. *Report of the Survey of the Public School System of the Town of Stamford, Connecticut.* 1922-23. Made by the Division of Field Studies, Institute of Educational Research. G. D. Strayer, Director, N. L. Engelhardt, Director in Charge of Survey. Teachers College, Columbia University, 1923.

UTICA, N. Y. *A Report of the Survey of the Utica School System.* State Department of Education, University of the State of N. Y. 1919.

WATERTOWN, N. Y. *Report of the Survey of the Schools of Watertown, New York.* School year 1924-25. Made by the Division of Field Studies, Institute of Educational Research. Teachers College Columbia University. G. D. Strayer, Director, N. L. Engelhardt, Asst. Director.

WHEELING, W. Va. *Educational Survey of Wheeling, West Virginia.* A Report of a Survey of the Public Schools of the Independent School District of Wheeling, W. Va. Made under the Direction of the U. S. Commissioner of Education. U. S. Bureau of Education, Bulletin 1921, No. 28, Parts 1 and 2.

WILMINGTON, DEL. *Survey of the Schools of Wilmington, Delaware,* Parts 1 and 2. Made by the Commissioner of Education. U. S. Bureau of Education Bulletin 1921, No. 2.

WINSTON-SALEM, N. C. *A Study of the Winston-Salem Schools.* Lester A. Williams. 1918.

VITA

Grover Cleveland Morehart: born at Lithopolis, Ohio, January 13, 1885; received the B.A. and M.A. degrees from Ohio State University, 1908 and 1921, respectively; admitted to the Montana Bar, 1913; a graduate student in Teachers College, Columbia University, New York City, 1922-23; a member of the Syracuse City Board of Education since January 1, 1926; a member of the New York State Governor's Commission on School Finance and Administration, 1925-26; Associate Professor of Education, Teachers College, Syracuse University, New York, 1923—.